PRAYER WARRIORS

# PRAYER WARRIORS

POWERFUL PORTRAITS
OF SOLDIER SAINTS
ON GOD'S FRONT LINES

A.W. Tozer
Holy Ann
Thomas Haire
E. D. Whiteside

**Christian Publications**
CAMP HILL, PENNSYLVANIA

Christian Publications, Inc.
3825 Hartzdale Drive, Camp Hill, PA 17011
www.cpi-horizon.com

*Faithful, biblical publishing since 1883*

ISBN: 0-87509-702-2

© 1998 by Christian Publications, Inc.

98  99  00  01  02    5  4  3  2  1

Unless otherwise indicated,
Scripture taken from the
HOLY BIBLE:
KING JAMES VERSION.

Some biographical material is adapted
from Robert L. Niklaus, John S. Sawin,
Samuel J. Stoesz, *All for Jesus*
(Christian Publications, 1986).

# Contents

# Preface

The story was told in *The Gospel Herald* of a British soldier who was caught one night creeping back to his quarters from the nearby woods. Taken before his commanding officer, he was charged with holding communications with the enemy. The man pleaded he had gone into the woods to pray by himself. That was his only defense.

"Down on your knees and pray now!" roared the officer. "You never needed it so much!"

Expecting immediate death, the soldier knelt and poured out his soul in eloquent prayer.

"You may go," said the officer simply when the soldier had finished. "I believe your story. If you hadn't drilled so often, you could not do so well at review."[1]

*Prayer Warriors* contains the stories of a number of soldiers of the Lord who have "drilled" in prayer often, who have battled in intercession and have come out victorious.

Along with marvelous answers to prayer, you will find among its pages various principles of an effective prayer life. Whether stated outright or demonstrated through example, these principles can help you fulfill your ministry of intercession and become a victorious warrior as well.

Prepare to be inspired, encouraged and challenged to join the fray!

David E. Fessenden
Managing Editor
Christian Publications, Inc.

[1]Lloyd Cory, *Quote, Unquote* (Wheaton, IL: Victor Books, 1977), 249.

## HOLY ANN

### An Irish Saint

*The following story of a faithful—yet very human—prayer warrior comes from* An Irish Saint (Holy Ann) *by Helen Bingham, now out of print.*

Ann Preston was born in the early 1800s to a humble family living in a small village in Ireland. Neither her father nor mother were inclined to religious matters, so Ann had no such training during much of her childhood. There was an attempt to give her some schooling, but Ann was there for no more than a week before she frustrated her teacher as a result of her slowness.

Because of her seeming inability to learn, Ann was hired to work for a nearby family and moved in with them. This family was not prone to religion either and had problems with liquor. One lady felt sorry for Ann and attempted to give her some religious training. She, like the teacher, gave up on Ann because of her ignorance.

After four years of working for this family, Ann went to work for a Christian lady who, after some poking and prodding, succeeded in getting Ann to accompany her to religious meetings. Though turned off at the start, Ann eventually gave her life to Christ under the preaching of Mr. Armstrong Halliday. Shortly after this, Ann was discharged from that job and went to work for the Reid family, with whom she moved overseas to Canada and stayed for many years.

Her early Christian experience was typical of a young child of God. It was based on the rise and fall of emotions, and there was much struggle between the flesh and the Spirit. Ann's particular hang-up was her Irish temper. There finally came a time where she became very frustrated with her inconsistencies. She wrestled with God as Jacob did about this very issue and came out with a promise of victory over her struggles. From that point on, Ann experienced such an indescribable joy and confidence in God that the people around her began to call her "Holy Ann."

Every life with which she came into contact was touched by her childlike faith in her heavenly Father to provide every need. Nothing was too small or too great for prayer. From finding lost articles of clothing to healing of the sick, Ann sent her prayers heaven-ward. Because of her simple yet unwavering faith in her Father and the intimate relationship that they shared, each prayer was answered and visible results were made evident.

Ann lived this way until her death at age ninety-six. There were many friends, some who came from many miles, and pastors in attendance at her funeral. All were there as a result of Ann's life, lived as a testimony to her Father.

By no means was Ann a well-known, highly regarded person by earthly standards. In heaven's eyes, however, her life was applauded as an example, then and now, of the love and faithfulness of God our Father.

## Power in Prayer

*"Whatsoever we ask, we receive of him, because we keep his commandments, and do those things that are pleasing in his sight."—1 John 3:22*

This poor, ignorant woman had stepped from a life of struggling, marked too often by defeat, into a life of power and blessing—power not only manward, but into a life of wonderful intimacy with God and prevailing prayer. It was not long before this became generally recognized and weaker Christians sought her counsel and begged her prayers, for it was very plainly seen that she had entered into the place where in a marvelous way she could "ask and receive," and where she had become a special subject of the thoughtful care of her heavenly Father.

There was one incident that she often told which in some directions has been received with doubt and skeptical unbelief, which beautifully illustrates this. We are confident that the facts are just as narrated.

In jumping over a fence she twisted her foot and injured the ankle. It got worse and worse, until finally she was unable to keep going around any longer. Dr. Reid said it would be necessary to scrape the bone. In these days, when such care is taken to relieve pain, we wonder how it was possible that Ann submitted to this painful operation without any anesthetic, but, as she said, the Lord sustained her. It was a long, long time before the wound healed, and for over a year Ann was unable to walk.

During this time of enforced inactivity she learned many precious lessons. She had become very weak through the great strain upon her system, and one day the doctor ordered her fresh eggs and milk. It did not occur to him that he was giving an impossible prescription, for it was in the dead of winter, and not a fresh egg was to be had anywhere in the village. All these matters were made subjects of prayer by Ann, who was learning already that the things impossible with man are possible with God.

She was sitting in her chair shortly after this, between the kitchen door and the back stairway. The door having been left ajar, to her surprise a hen came in and dropped down at Ann's feet. Something said to her, "Lift it up and put it on the first step of the stair." Intuitively Ann recognized that her Father was about to meet her need. The hen went upstairs, and in her simple way Ann asked that it might not be permitted to cackle, lest Dr. Reid's daughters should hear it. (In the village at that time there was another unique character who was the laughingstock of the boys because she permitted the hens to live in her house, and Ann did not want to be likened to old Peggy Casey.) After a few minutes the hen came down very quietly and Ann reached to the door and let her out.

Then another great difficulty faced her. She had not put any weight on her foot for a long time. It was impossible for her to walk, and while she was confident that the doctor's prescription had been filled at the top of the stairs, she did not know how she was to obtain it. She prayed, and felt that the answer came, "Go up for it." But in her simple way she said, "Father, how can I? It is impossible." Some time before this she had learned a little refrain which she had taken as one of the motto verses of her life. It ran like this:

Faith, mighty faith, the promise sees
    And looks to God alone,
Laughs at impossibilities
    And cries, "It shall be done."

When she spoke of impossibilities the inward voice said, "Well, say your verse." She hesitated for some time, but at last faith conquered and she repeated the simple words. Then she received her instructions as to how she was to act. She worked her chair toward the door, and then, sitting on the first step, she raised herself with her hands, step after step, until she had reached the top. The hen had laid the egg in an old box just at the head of the stair, and she was able to reach it without getting off the top step. But how was she to get down with the egg in her hand? In her simple way—for she used to pray about all these little things in a very familiar manner—she asked for directions, and the word came, "Put it in your pocket." She then managed to descend in the same fashion, and was just safely back in her chair when Paddy, the servant, walked in. Ann prayed, "Now, Father, don't let him ask me where I got it," and in response to her simple faith he took the egg without a word and fixed it for her without making any inquiry. This is the more surprising when it is stated that he had been all through the village in his endeavor to secure eggs for Ann.

For three weeks the hen returned every day without making the slightest noise. At the end of this time the doctor one morning said she did not need any more milk and eggs and recommended beef tea instead. Just after this a lady came in, and the hen, disturbed, came cackling downstairs. The young woman was very much startled, and said, "What, Ann, have you got hens upstairs like old Peggy Casey?" And as the hen came cackling down, the young girl shooed it out into the yard and it never returned. Afterward when Ann was able to get out again she tried to single out this one in order to show it special kindness, but was unable to do so. When in her customary way she appealed to her Father to show her which one it was, she heard the voice speaking to her inward conscious-ness, and telling her, "My glory will I not give to an-other." For a long time Ann hesitated to speak of this incident, but her diffidence in telling of God's good-ness was reproved, for she heard Him say, "I fed you just as really as I fed Elijah through the ravens, and yet you are ashamed to make it known."

Some time after her experience with the hen Ann was away from home visiting some friends in the country. She ventured to tell them how her Father had provided for her in her sickness. The lady of the house expressed her unbelief, but Ann said quietly, "Well, my Father will make you believe it before I go." And sure enough He did.

Ann had not the money to take her home, and one morning as she knelt in prayer she asked her Father how much it would cost, and had just received the an-swer when the door opened and the lady of the house stood there. Ann said, "Oh, come in, till I see if you can count as well as my Father." She came in and reckoned up the mileage and what the fare would be, and it was exactly the same amount as that which Ann had been told. Then the woman said, "Do you think you will get it, Ann?" She replied, "To be sure I shall. I am sure of it, for the silver and the gold are my Fa-ther's and the cattle upon a thousand hills, and I am sure He will send it to me."

That morning she started out with the woman's mother to spend the day. She had only been away about half an hour when a man called and asked for the "shouting girl." The woman said, "She has just gone out for the day," and then she added in an un-usual way, "Do you know, she was praying this morning for money to take her back home, and she says she is sure her Father will send it." "Well," said the man, "and so am I, for I have it here in my pocket." He then told her how he had been impressed to give her the amount, and had been sent around with it. The woman was astonished, and when she saw Ann returning that evening she ran out to meet her and at once proceeded to tell her the good news. In a quiet, matter-of-fact way Ann said, "Didn't I tell you? I knew my Father would send it to me. You remember you wouldn't believe about the egg, and I told you my Father would make you believe before I left. So now this has come for you." In order to avoid the point of the remark the woman said, "Well, give me the money then, if it has come for me," but quickly Ann replied, "No, the money was sent for me, but the lesson is for you."

It must not be thought, however, that Ann's prayers were always selfish. She had a large heart for the needs of others. Every spring she used to make two barrels of soft soap—one for their own use and always one for the poor. On one occasion she had made the one barrelful and was at the last kettleful of the second, when something seemed to go wrong and it would not thicken. The children came out to see how she was getting along, and of course, childlike, they wanted to know what was the matter with the soap. In her familiar way Ann said, "My Father says it only needs a bone." They asked, "Well, haven't you got one?" She said, "No, but my Father bids me wait till morning." "But suppose it should rain in the night? The water would spoil it more." But Ann quietly said, "My Father said wait till the morning, and I will wait, and cover it up now."

By 3 o'clock the next morning Ann was up and out to see her soap. There by the side of the kettle lay a large marrow bone, from which the meat had all been taken, but which had not been boiled. With her quiet "Thank You," Ann lifted up her heart in praise, and then picking up the ax, proceeded to break the bone and put it in the soap, and in a short time it had the desired effect.

The children were very anxious to see the outcome of Ann's faith. Her calm confidence in these matters had already produced an effect in the home, and they somehow expected to see Ann's prayers answered. When, in reply to their query, she said that the bone had come, "It was here by the kettle when I came out," one of the children said, "Oh, I guess a dog dropped the bone there." Like a flash Ann retorted, "I don't care if the devil brought it; my Father sent it."

To show her interest and sympathy with others, another incident is told which was well verified at the time. The Salvation Army had opened up a station in the village and Ann became interested in them. She found on inquiry that the officers in charge were really in actual need. She asked some friends with whom she was staying if they ever took them in any food. They replied that they had on several occasions but added, "We haven't very much to give." Ann asked the woman if she would not take them some eggs, but the response was that the hens were not laying then. Ann said, "Well, but if I ask my Father for them, will you give them to the officers?" The woman replied, "Yes, I will."

Ann went to prayer, and shortly afterward she proceeded to the barn and gathered over a dozen eggs. The woman was amazed and wanted to know where she got them, but Ann would not satisfy her curiosity in the matter. As bearing upon this incident, it is a significant fact that this woman years afterward sent in to the city to request Ann's prayers.

Of course, in many of these incidents one may find a natural explanation, and we are not trying to narrate these experiences with the thought that a miracle was wrought in every instance. God frequently uses natural things in order to answer the prayers of His children. Of course, some may say that the things all happened by chance, but it is certainly a most convenient chance that always appears to meet the needs of those who cry unto God.

Ann tells how, shortly after she was able to get around after her long sickness, when she was still using her crutches somewhat, and it was most difficult to get to meetings, special services were started in the church. She sought to get out on every occasion. She was always eager to assist and ever anxious to lead souls to Christ. One morning when Ann got up, to her dismay she noticed that there had been a heavy fall of snow. She at once said, "O Father, now I can't go to the meeting tonight. Won't You please send someone to make a path for me?" At that time there was no man in the house, and the building was nearly a quarter of a mile back from the road. On several other occasions, in answer to her prayers, someone had been sent along to shovel snow, but this day, after Ann's prayer, she heard the girls laughing, and one said to the other, "Come and see what is making the path for Ann." When Ann looked out there were five horses going up the avenue one after the other as straight as a line. They ran up and down in colt fashion no less than four times, until there was a perfectly beaten track all through the deep snow. As soon as they got out on the road, however, they began to scatter, but up the avenue they had made a regular, straight track. Ann told how she enjoyed the meeting that night, and to those who gathered there told with beaming face how God had opened her way through the snow.

## The Story of the Well

> "He . . . gave them drink, as out of the great depths."—Psalm 78:15

One of the most remarkable answers to prayer in Ann's experience was that in which she obtained water in a dry well. This incident has been told and retold scores of times, with all sorts of variations and additions. I was most careful to get the full particulars and surrounding circumstances taken down as Ann narrated it. The event occurred in the long, dry weeks of summer. During this period the well at their home was usually dry for two or three months, and the boys were compelled to haul water in barrels from the well about half a mile away. This was very hard work, especially when they had to provide not only for household needs, but for the stock as well. One evening at the close of the day Ann was sitting in the kitchen with the boys around her, telling them some of the remarkable ways in which her heavenly Father had answered her prayers. When she had just concluded one of these narratives, Henry said, "Ann, why don't you ask your Father to send water in that well and not have us boys work so hard? I was down in the well looking at it today, and it is just as dry as the floor." This was thrown out to Ann in a half-joking, half-earnest way, as though to challenge her faith. He little dreamt of the serious way that Ann would take it.

When she got up into her little room that night she knelt in prayer and said, "Now, Father, You heard what Henry said tonight. If I get up in class meeting and say, 'My God shall supply all your needs according to his riches in glory by Christ Jesus,' the boys won't believe I am what I profess to be if You don't send the water in the well." She then continued to plead that the water might be sent, and finally, rising from her knees, she said, "Now, Father, if I am what I profess to be, there will be water in the well in the morning."

When she came down the next morning Henry was out preparing to go for the water as usual. To his surprise and great amusement he saw Ann take up the two pails and start for the well. He watched her from the kitchen window as she hooked the pail to the windlass and began to lower it. If she had done it the night before it would have gone with a bang to the bottom, but after a while there was a splash, and still down the pail went. Ann began with difficulty to wind up the windlass again, and at last put the pail upon the well-stand full of water. She repeated this and with both pails full of clear, sparkling water, she walked up to the house.

And who could wonder that there was a little air of victory as she set down the pails and said to Henry, "Well, what do you say now?" To her surprise he simply answered, "Well, why didn't you do that long ago, and save us all that work?" Meditation upon that question, thrown out so thoughtlessly by this young boy, might yield some very profitable results. How often we go hungry and thirsty, suffering the lack of all sorts of needed things, when a full supply might be ours! "Ye have not, because ye ask not" (James 4:2). Years after a friend visited the well and was told that from the time referred to the well had never been known to be dry summer or winter.

## Linking Divine Knowledge with Earthly Need

> *"What things soever ye desire, when ye pray, believe that ye receive them, and ye shall have them."*—Mark 11:24

It will be impossible for many Christians to understand the intimacy and familiarity with which Ann addressed the Divine Being. To some it will sound almost irreverent—we question whether there are not those who would think it blasphemous to speak in the simple way that Ann was accustomed to do of her heavenly Father. Further, we know there are those who would protest against bringing the thousand and one little matters of everyday life into the sphere of prayer. It was quite a common thing for Ann to go around at her daily tasks talking as familiarly to the heavenly Father about every little thing as she would talk to any other person that might be in the home. Moreover, she sought guidance in every little detail of life.

That she received special answers, those who lived with her have no doubt. Even the children in their play would run to Ann for a solution for the little difficulties that arose. One of the boys on one occasion had lost a spade and was dreading the wrath of his father when he should discover that the article was missing. In his distress he went to Ann and appealed to her to ask her Father about it. She at once in her simple way closed her eyes and said, "Father, where is it?" We cannot explain how she understood, or in what form these answers made themselves known to her consciousness, but she immediately made a beeline for the back of the garden where the spade was lying hidden in the grass. This was not by any means an isolated case. The children would come to her when their toys were lost and invariably after Ann had prayed she would at once go to where the missing article was lying.

Only on one occasion did she fail to get her answer about such things, and this exception happened thus: a young minister was visiting the home and was out on the lawn playing croquet with the girls. Ann did not approve of this; at least she did not think it was right for the minister to be spending his time in that way. In her blunt way she asked if he could keep his mind stayed upon God while he was doing this. He replied, "Oh, yes, for a little while." As the game proceeded, one of the young ladies lost a much-prized locket. However, she was quite unconcerned and said, "Oh, never mind. Ann will soon find it for me." She came in and said, "Ann, get it for me now, quick." Ann, in her usual way, went to her Father, but no answer came. She went out to look for it, but could not find it, and it was never found.

Many, many years after she had left the Reid family she came to live at our home. The boys had heard a great deal about Ann's wonderful experiences, and naturally expected to see some demonstration. They hardly liked at first to ask Ann to demonstrate these things, but they used to hide things which Ann would need to use, and then watch to see how she would find them. Perhaps some article of clothing would be put in the most out-of-the-way place they could think of, and then they would watch for the time when Ann would need to use it.

Being perfectly ignorant of what had occurred, she would go up to her room or walk up to a corner with her eyes closed, and in her simple way she would say, "Father, where is it?" and after standing a moment or two in silence she would turn around and go directly to the spot where the thing was hidden. We do not profess to explain this; we simply narrate what has occurred over and over again. At one place the boys hid the cat and Ann was asked where it was. She had no idea of what had been done, but in her simple way she looked up in prayer, and then made straight for the stove and opened the oven door, when the cat at once jumped out.

Of course in a Christian home such things would not occur very often to satisfy mere idle curiosity. It was not long before those who knew her felt it was too solemn a thing to be thus dealt with. However, in times of need there was never any question as to the fact of Ann's prayers being answered.

On one occasion she had risen in the morning, and, as usual, had asked her Father for a verse with which to start the day. The special portion that was given to her was, "And we know that all things work together for good to them that love God" (Romans 8:28). It came while they were at family prayer and Ann said, "And we will see it before night, too. God will show it." All through the day Ann watched, but nothing unusual happened.

However, when the girls returned from meeting that night Ann asked if they had had a good meeting. One of them answered, "Why, how could we when I lost all the money I had to live on next week on the way there?" Then they told how the money had been lost and they had looked for it all the evening with a lantern. Before they retired, at the family altar Ann reminded her Father of the promise of the morning and asked that He would keep the money for her wherever it was. Early in the morning she was wakened with the instruction, "Arise and get the money that you gave Me to keep for you last night." Then came the other voice: "Nonsense! Your leg is too bad for you to get up and go." She did not obey at once and was just falling to sleep when again the voice spoke, bidding her to arise. She went out and walked down the path, not looking specially for it, but all at once she was stopped by her Father and she saw a bill lying almost hidden with the snow by the side of a small hill.

She picked it up and took it across the road, where her friend, Mrs. Hughes, lived. Rapping at the door, she said, "Get up and see if this is a bill." The lady took the bill and looked at it in amazement, and said, "This is a $5 bill." Ann said, "Come and let us praise the Lord for this." After prayer Ann went back home and going in, threw the bill down and said, "There; there is your money." The girls looked at it in surprise, for they had searched so long for it. Then they said, "Oh Ann, don't tell it in class meeting, or people will think we were so careless."

# 2

**THOMAS HAIRE**

# The Praying Plumber of Lisburn

*The following chapter is taken from "Thomas Haire: The Praying Plumber of Lisburn" by A.W. Tozer now out of print. The last section, though part of Tozer's booklet, was written by Thomas Haire himself.*

By a remarkable providence this sketch of Tom Haire by A.W. Tozer brings together two men who in most ways are very much different but who in their affinity for things spiritual are very much alike. Accordingly, they have another characteristic in common: Both are nonconformists, each fashioned by divine processes according to an individual pattern.

The significance of God-made men in the twentieth-century West can best be appreciated against the backdrop of our times. In this age of mass production and mass media of communication, when the stress in school and church, at least in America, is on social adjustment, the inevitable result is mediocre conformity. The product is a religious robot instead of a saint. "This world is not a friend to grace" takes on added meaning in our day, and it helps to explain why there are so few saintly Christians.

The orders of the Catholic Church have for centuries tried to produce saints by imposing a right regimentation of thoughts and conduct on the human spirit. While few Protestant groups have followed this procedure, the prevalent insistence on group conformity is just as deadly. The liberal can be identified by an affected intonation and a repetition of liberal clichés. The fundamentalist, indoctrinated in a particular school of orthodoxy, becomes an acceptable poll-parrot of verbalism. Even "holiness" preachers have their characteristic mode of expression—their badge of the spiritually elite.

The human spirit, however, can only be repressed by this insistence on social conformity. It is a tragic misuse of freedom to use it for even the more refined types of enslavement. It must be set free by Christian redemption and servitude to Jesus Christ to find its realization in the boundless reaches of the eternal. Fortunately, neither the subject nor the author of this sketch is a product of convention. Had either been so there would be no sketch, for there would have been nothing to write about on the one hand, and on the other, the author would not have had the insight to appreciate the spiritual stature of Tom Haire. Both were needed to produce this kindred spirit of Dr. Tozer speaking through his gifted pen.

How the plumber from Lisburn, Ireland and the editor of *The Alliance Weekly* (now *Alliance Life*) in Chicago were brought into an intimate understanding of one another is an extraordinary providence. The hotel fire that almost took the lives of Tom Haire and Evangelist Ravenhill is one link in a chain forged by divine purpose. How fellowship in things spiritual is gloriously possible is here demonstrated. Tom Haire, the layman, has little formal education while the author's learning extends to many fields, but in very different ways they are God-made men whose habitat is the heavenlies, where both are very much at home.

It has been my good fortune to know both the author and the subject of these chapters. Both men are enemies of exaggeration, pretense, sensationalism and window dressing. Accordingly, this sketch is an honest account, and I earnestly pray that it will be used of God to bring many of His children into a closer fellowship with Himself.

One of the rarest experiences I have ever had was in prayer with Tom Haire. As his hands clasped my hand with that of a distinguished churchman and theologian, he poured out his heart in prolonged intercession. Afterward, the prelate and I agreed that this kind of prayer in its depth and height and breadth and insight was outside any human dimensions. Tom had not learned to pray in any school of human tutoring. We had been listening to a man converse with God who knew from the Spirit's tutoring the concerns of the Father's heart and the vocabulary of the heavenlies.

Dr. S.A. Witmer, President<br>Fort Wayne Bible College

## An Irishman with a Heart for God

You have only to glance at his round red face and his twinkling blue eyes to guess the place of his birth. And when he smiles and says, "Guid marnin'," there is no doubt left. Tom Haire is Irish.

Tom is not just somewhat Irish; he is so completely identified with the looks and ways and speech of the Emerald Isle that nothing on earth can ever change him. His soft, thick, almost fuzzy brogue reminds you of every Pat-and-Mike story you have ever heard, and the happy upside-down construction that often comes out when he talks sounds like the best of John M. Synge. It would take a keener ear than mine and greater literary skill than I possess to hear and reproduce in print the delightful if sometimes confusing dialect which is the only language Tom knows and in which he clothes his deeply spiritual and penetrating observations. So, except for an occasional Hibernicism in word or phrase which I consider too good to pass up, I shall make no attempt to copy his Irish speech. For the purposes of this sketch I shall let Tom speak

22

in ordinary American English, though I admit we may lose something by so doing.

It is not with Tom Haire the Irishman that we are concerned here, however, but with Brother Tom Haire, the servant of Christ. So fully has he lost himself in God that the text "Not I, but Christ" actually seems to be a reality in his life. I think I have never heard him quote the text, but his whole being is a living exemplification of it. He appears to live the text each moment of each day.

After two years of growing acquaintance with and increasing appreciation of this man of faith I concluded that I owed it to the Christian public to share with them some of the good things God has given me through His servant Tom Haire. I have long felt and still feel that the practice of writing up living men and spreading them before the public is questionable. It is especially bad when new converts are seized upon as gospel propaganda and paraded before the world as evidences of the truth of the Christian religion. Converted cowboys, opera stars and such have so completely captured the attention of the Christian public that it has become increasingly difficult to hold a sober view of the faith of our fathers. I do not want to contribute to this delinquency in any form, but I felt that a man who has been praying for fifty years as Tom has, and whose long godly life has been open to critical examination for that time, was safe material for a brief write-up. And besides, Tom is just a plumber, not a celebrity, so any interest he may arouse among Christians is bound to be spiritual.

After Tom is gone someone will undoubtedly write a book about him. In the meantime, there are thousands of persons who might profit by knowing something of his life and teachings now. So low has the level of spirituality fallen among the churches that it is imperative that every effort possible be made to raise it. One effective way to inspire Christians to press onward into the deep things of God is to show them that there are a few saintly souls among us even now, in whom the complexities and iniquities of the twentieth century have not wholly destroyed the art of prayer and spiritual communion of a biblical quality. This knowledge may easily do more to encourage men and women in the pursuit of God than a thousand sermons could do.

When we consider how quick Christ and His apostles were to focus attention upon persons who were spiritually worthy, and that we are admonished in the Scriptures to emulate those who have risen to a place of unusual faith and godliness, there would seem to be no valid reason to withhold this sketch any longer. Tom will not see what is written until it appears in print; and if I know him as well as I believe I do he will not read it afterward. Tom is like that.

After I had become convinced that something should be written about Tom, the next problem was to persuade him to agree to it. And that was not easy. When I broached the subject to him he demurred immediately. "They wanted to send reporters out to talk to me," he said, "but I wouldn't let them. I am only a plumber. All I have is from God and I don't want to

24

let any man elevate me in any way." Then his red face became redder still, his eyes filled with tears and his voice got husky. "I'm afraid of losing me power with God," he whispered.

After I had explained to him that I felt he owed a debt to other Christians to let them know how good the Lord had been to him and had promised that I would be careful to give him no glory or credit at all, Tom felt better about the matter and agreed to talk to me. Especially was he touched by the argument that he owed something to his fellow Christians. Tom loves God's people with a wonderful, radiant affection and is willing to do anything to bring a blessing to them.

Tom Haire was born sixty-six years ago in County Down, North Ireland ("Protestant Ireland," as Tom always carefully explains), and apart from two visits to the United States has lived all his life there. He is a member of the Episcopal Church of Ireland, the "disestablished" wing of the Episcopal Church whose worship is much simpler and less ornate than that of the Anglicans and which is evangelical in belief and evangelistic in spirit. He is a lay preacher and evangelist, but until recently stayed very close to Lisburn, his home, where his plumbing business is located. He was so busy with his business and his evangelistic work, he says with a twinkle, that he did not get around to finding a wife till he was thirty-nine years old. He has a married daughter, Margaret, whose husband now looks after Tom's business affairs. His wife has been dead for thirteen years.

The two characteristics that mark Tom Haire as un-usual are his utter devotion to prayer and his amazing spiritual penetration. (And are not the two always closely associated?) Three months after his conversion, when he was sixteen years old, he formed the habit of praying four hours each day. This practice he followed faithfully for many years. Later he added one all-night prayer session each week. In 1930 these weekly all-night times were increased to two, and in 1948 he settled down to the habit of praying three nights of every week. He gets along on very little sleep. In addition to the three nights each week that he stays awake to pray he is frequently awakened in the night seasons by a passage of Scripture or a burden of prayer that will not let him rest. "And almost always," he says, "the Lord wakens me early in the morning to pray."

## A Peaceful Heart

Tom Haire is a rare compound of deep, tender de-votion, amazing good sense and a delightful sense of humor. There is about him absolutely nothing of the tension found in so many persons who seek to live the spiritual life.

Tom is completely free in the Spirit and will not al-low himself to be brought under bondage to the rudi-ments of the world nor the consciences of other people. His attitude toward everyone and everything is one of good-natured tolerance if he does not like it or smiling approval if he does. The things he does not like he is sure to pray about, and the things he ap-proves he is sure to make matters of thanksgiving to

God. But always he is relaxed and free from strain. He will not allow himself to get righteously upset about anything. "I lie near to the heart of God," he says, "and I fear nothing in the world."

That he lies near to God's heart is more than a passing notion to Tom. It is all very real and practical. "God opens His heart," he says, "and takes us in. In God all things are beneath our feet. All power is given to us and we share God's almightiness." He has no confidence at all in mankind, but believes that God must be all in all. Not even our loftiest human desires or holiest prayers are acceptable to God. "The river flows from beneath the throne," he explains, "and its source is not of this world. So the source of our prayers must be Christ Himself hidden in our hearts."

Though he counts heavily on the power of prayer he has no faith in the virtue of prayer itself as such. He warns against what he calls "merit prayer" by which he means any prayer offered with the secret notion that there is something good in it which will impress God and which He must recognize and reward. Along with "merit prayer" goes "merit-faith," which is the faith we think will in some way please God.

"Too many of God's people are straining for faith," says Tom, "and holding on hard trying to exercise it. This will never do at all. The flesh cannot believe no matter how hard it tries, and we only wear ourselves out with our human efforts. True faith is the gift of God to an obedient soul and comes of itself without effort. The source of faith is Christ in us. It is a fruit of the Spirit."

He flatly rejects the notion that we "can buy something with prayer." "God's gifts come from another source," he insists. "They are 'freely given' and have no price attached. It is the goodness of God that gives us all things. God gives His free gifts generously to those of His children who bring themselves into harmony with His will. Then they have but to ask and He gives."

Brother Tom fasts quite often and sometimes the fast is prolonged for some time. But he scorns the thought that there is any merit in it. "Some people," says Tom with a shake of the head, "some people half kill themselves by ascetic practices. They imagine God to be so severe that He enjoys seeing them hungry. They go about pale and weak in the mistaken belief that they are making themselves dear to God. All such notions come from the flesh and are false." Once during a prolonged season of prayer he got suddenly thirsty and without a qualm of conscience broke off prayer and went out for a cup of tea. This got him into difficulties with certain fellow Christians who felt that he was surrendering to fleshly appetites. But he has dwelt so long in the spacious heart of God that he is unaffected by the scruples of others. God's heart is no strait jacket even if some imperfectly taught saints insist on acting as if it were. "Where the Spirit of the Lord is, there is liberty."

Wherever there is a strain in the life we may be sure the flesh is operating. The Holy Spirit gives fruitful burdens but never brings strain. Our very eagerness to have our prayers answered may cause us to lapse into

28

the flesh if we are not watchful. So Tom reasons. A woman sent for him recently and wanted him to pray for her healing. She was in very bad condition, but Tom would not pray. He detected in her eagerness to get well a bit of rebellion against the will of God. So he set about breaking her rebellion down. "Sister," he asked innocently, "and have you ever read the Scripture, 'Precious in the sight of the Lord is the death of his saints'? Sure, and you would not want to rob the Lord of all that preciousness, would you?" It was his way of telling her that she was not fit to live unless she was willing to die. The shock had its intended effect, and after some further conversation Tom felt that the woman had surrendered her will to God. Then he prayed for her healing. She received some help physically, and in addition she had also the benefit that comes from a new spiritual experience.

Tom holds back from the highly advertised healing meeting, but he ardently believes that an outpouring of the Holy Spirit on a life may easily result in physical healing. "Should God ever pour out His Spirit again upon all flesh," he says, "we may expect physical healings to accompany the outpouring. It is part of the divine pattern."

Tom's conception of prayer is so lofty and so different from the popular conception as to be something of another order entirely. To him prayer is a spiritual art, subject to divine laws which must be obeyed if our prayers are to achieve success. "Harmony" and "dominion" are two words that come easily from his lips when talking about prayer. Once in a sermon I spoke of God's making man in His image. At the close of the service Tom spoke a word of approval of the sermon and then went on to develop the thought further. He called attention to the words occurring so close together, "image" and "dominion." "Do you notice," he asked, "how God made man in His own image and then gave him dominion? The dominion followed the image, and so it is with us now. Our dominion in prayer depends upon how much of the image of God we carry in our hearts. There must be complete harmony between the soul and God if we are to enjoy answered prayer. The degree of success we enjoy in prayer depends upon the image within us." Then he added a significant sentence: "For instance, God would not hear a man who would kick a dog."

## A Charitable Heart

Tom Haire, on the whole, takes a very charitable attitude toward all his fellow Christians and toward every shade of doctrinal belief within the framework of evangelical Christianity.

He would not be classified as a teacher of divine healing but he has strong convictions about the believer's privileges in Christ as they touch his physical body. He believes that God sometimes gives a praying man the assurance of healing for someone else. "There is a sense in which a true Christian may receive healing for another," he says, "God using him as a channel through which He can pour Himself out upon the needy person." In Tom's theology the onus of failure when praying for the sick never falls upon the sick man. Those who do the praying are responsible to exercise faith for the one in need. That is quite a reversal of the current practice of heaping scorn upon the sick man because he cannot get up after he has been prayed for.

In prayer we need always to obtain the wisdom of the Spirit so that we may pray according to the will of God and not suffer discouragement from failure to see our desires realized. "When I get the mind of God," Tom insists, "I always get the answer. When the wisdom of God floods over my understanding I can take the sick man by the hand and tell him to get up."

But even here he will not allow himself to get under bondage. He seeks not to support a doctrinal bias but to discover and follow the will of God. He tells of praying once for the recovery of a Christian woman who he felt was greatly needed on earth. He was on his knees interceding for her when he felt a check on his spirit. Then he thought he heard the Lord speaking in his heart. "Don't pray for her, Tom," the voice seemed to say. "I have prepared a big reception for her up here. I want her with Me." Tom immediately ceased to pray and began to celebrate the blessed reception about to be held in heaven for the departing sister. Shortly after this she went to be with Christ.

Brother Tom's prayer list is very long and contains among other things the names of many persons for whom he makes regular intercession. Once when going over his list before the Lord he came to the name of a dear friend who had lately died. "Being a Protestant," says Tom, "I took out me pencil and started to cross off his name, for I did not believe in praying for the dead. But the Lord spoke to me and said, 'No, Tom, do not cross him off. Just write after his name the word *Home*! You have not lost him!' " Tom happily obeyed, and while he did not again intercede for his friend, he never felt that he had died. The relationship between these two Christians had not been altered by the mere incident of death. This world and the one above are never far apart and sometimes they actually touch and intermingle. This has been the comforting belief of the sweetest saints of the ages, and Tom's experiences only seem to confirm the truth.

Anything that begins or ends in *self* is extremely hateful to Tom Haire. Self-righteousness, self-confidence and every other self-sin must be slain within us if we are to grow in the love of God. He goes back to the sixth chapter of Romans for his theology and insists that the doctrine become real in the life. To Tom the sanctified life is one that is dead indeed unto sin and alive unto God through Christ Jesus.

"A man is dead," he says, "when he no longer resists the will of God in anything. Dead men do not resist. You must go to God as a lamb, to obey, follow and die." Brother Tom sees a close relationship between dying and giving. "We must come to God with our hands open. A man can't be crucified while he keeps his fists closed. Open your hands in generous giving and hold nothing back. Even tithing can be harmful if we unconsciously feel that the one tenth we have given is all that belongs to God. *Everything* is His; we own nothing at all. The tenth is only the amount we set aside for religious work. The other nine-tenths are His also, but He graciously permits us to use it as we have need."

When Tom was a young man God filled him with the Holy Ghost and he has never forgotten it. But he does not rest upon an experience that happened so long ago. He believes that we should go on to be filled again and again as the need arises. "If I am filled in 1953," he explains, "in 1954 there will be new areas discovered in my life of which I was unaware. These, too, need to be filled and claimed for God by the sovereign Holy Ghost."

While discussing the doctrine and experience of the Holy Spirit with him I took occasion to inquire what he thought of the notion that everyone who is filled with the Spirit will speak in tongues. I knew that his views would be of great value because they spring out of fifty years of holy living and victorious praying. Here would be no mere theory nor prejudiced opinion, but a wise and spiritual word spoken out of long familiarity with the Holy Ghost.

To my blunt question, "Brother Tom, have you ever spoken with tongues?" he gave the answer smilingly and gently: "No. I have never spoken in tongues, but I do not 'forbid' anyone from doing so. I think, however, that I have been instrumental in leading many persons from tongues to love. You see, I do not need tongues. I can make myself clear to others with the one I have now, and God knows what I am saying before I utter a word. So of what use would tongues be to me?" It may be that someone has spoken a wiser word on this controversial subject, but if so I have not heard it.

## Hating the Sin But Not the Sinner

For sinners and for defeated Christians Tom Haire feels only pity and a great sorrow of heart, but toward sin itself his attitude is one of stern, unsmiling hostility. To him sin is the cause of all our human woe, the veil that shuts us out from the blessed presence of God. It is never to be tolerated in any form by anyone who wishes to follow Christ.

From his view of sin it naturally follows that he holds repentance to be indispensable to salvation. His usually mild language becomes sharp and imperious as he calls his hearers to forsake iniquity and turn to God. For him there can be no compromise with wrongdoing. The seeking heart must make its eternal choice, either to serve sin and suffer the everlasting displeasure of God or to forsake all sin and enter into the divine fellowship through the mercies of Christ.

If you were to ask Tom what he considers the greatest hindrance to prayer he would answer instantly, "unconfessed sin." And in coming to God the first thing to deal with is sin in the life. But for all that, it never enters his mind that he can atone for his sins by any kind of penance or self-punishment. Forgiveness is a free gift of God based upon the work of Christ on the cross and is never to be had on any other terms than faith. When a sin has been forsaken and confessed it is at that moment forgiven, never to be remembered against us forever. No possible good can come from brooding over it. It is gone for good.

Learned theologians have a fancy name for the doctrine of sin. They call it "hamartiology." In all probability Tom would not recognize the word if he chanced to come upon it, but his own hamartiology is fully adequate. He likes to recall that with God, forgiving and forgetting are the same thing. When God forgives, he forgets. Then Tom sums up his joyous personal theology in a single sentence, "If God forgets," he asks happily, "why should I remumber?"

Tom has made two visits to the United States within the last few years. As he approached our shores for the first time he hid himself away on board the ship and sought the face of God in great earnestness to know what he should say to the "Amuricans." What God said to him, or what he seemed to hear God say to him, was so deep and wise that it should be seriously studied by every one of us. Whether it was the very voice of God or only the crystallization of a wisdom that had come to him through long years of praying matters not at all. It is too wise and wonderful to ignore.

"When you get to America," the Voice said within him, "don't get mixed up in doctrinal trifles. Don't pay any attention to their heads. Just look at their hearts. You will find their differences to be of the head; their similarities to be of the heart. So talk to their hearts. Don't read up on the religious situation in America. Don't try to fit into things or please people. Just talk to them straight out of your heart. Tell them the things I have told you, and you will get on all right." Fortunately Tom had the courage and good sense to obey these wise admonitions.

Tom Haire, like many other uneducated men, takes an attitude of meek deference toward all learning, and gazes with great respect upon any man he considers learned. But his confidence in his own kind of learning makes him bold to speak out even in the presence of the great. "My knowledge," he says, "has been all on the experiential plane. I have never had the slightest interest in theology as a mere theory. There is an anointing which teaches all things so that we need not that any man teach us." This attitude he holds in complete humility without bigotry and without arrogance. Once I talked to him about the views held by certain unbelieving intellectuals that seemed to contradict his views. He advanced no arguments to support his position. He bowed his head and spoke in a low voice: "But they've never been where I've been," he said simply.

I have not felt free to ask Tom outright what books he has read. I only know that I have never seen him with any book except the Bible. It is altogether safe to assume that he has not read any of the devotional writers of the ages, yet his whole spiritual outlook is that of an evangelical mystic. There is a catholicity about him that would have made him completely at home with the great saints of the past. He could have preached to the birds along with Francis of Assisi (though his practical Irish mind would likely have inquired, "Shure, and what is the guid of it all?"). He might have sung across England with Richard Rolle or sat in silence with George Fox or preached in a cemetery with John Wesley. And when the fiery logic of Charles Finney had devastated a congregation Tom might have come among the terrified seekers with his Bible and his wise words of instruction and led them straight to God.

The spiritual outlook of this twentieth-century Irishman is so near to that of the fourteenth-century Germans, Eckhart and Tauler, and the seventeenth-century Frenchman, Fenelon, as to create a suspicion that he may be indebted to their writings for many of his ideas. But such is positively not the case. In all our dozens of conversations and our long prayer seasons together he has never so much as mentioned their names, nor has he ever quoted from their writings so much as one sentence. To him they simply do not exist. The only explanation for the remarkable resemblance between these Christian men so far removed in time is that the same Holy Spirit taught all of them, and where He can find listening ears He always teaches the same things. There is a unity of spiritual beliefs among men of the Spirit that jumps centuries, denominational gulfs and doctrinal hedges and perfects a communion of saints in spite of every effort of devil or man to keep them apart.

## A Man of Integrity

It is important to any proper understanding of the grace of God in the life of His servant, Thomas Haire, that we do not think of him as a plaster saint or as a mystic dreamer far removed from the rough and downright world where we live. He has not fled the world to escape it; better than flight has been his deliverance from it while living in the midst of it.

I have wanted to be altogether fair in presenting this sketch. To eulogize at the expense of accuracy would be to defeat the very end I am trying to attain, namely, to show what God can do for a man if the man will but place himself in His hands. Were the object of this sketch a perfect man the effect would be to discourage us completely. The pale wax saint who never knew human imperfections could not inspire us to godliness. Even Christ had to be tempted in all points like as we are, and the high priests of the temple must themselves be compassed with infirmity if they were to know how to have compassion on the ignorant and them that were out of the way.

It is my desire to present here both sides of the ledger, to show the credit side certainly, and then to exhibit the debit side to get a balanced picture.

Probably the best commentary on the life and character of God's Irish servant is to say that after two years of rather intimate acquaintance with him I am unable to dig up anything of any consequence to write on the debit side of his life. I have seen him in the most trying circumstances, undergoing tests that would have tried the character of an angel, and I have not in one single instance seen him act otherwise than like a Christian.

It was the doctrine of the Wesleyan theologians that a man can be perfected in love and yet be imperfect in other phases of his life, that perfect love does not necessarily imply perfect judgment. Tom Haire appears to me to be a fine proof of the truth of this doctrine. His glowing love for God and men, his utter devotion to prayer and praise, have yet left him open to errors of judgment much as any of us. He is the first one to mention this, and is keenly aware of the necessity to lean hard on God that he may be saved from serious mistakes.

For instance, Tom is much more generous with his affections than I could feel free to be, but in the light of the practices of godly men and women of the past and the admonitions of the Scriptures concerning the holy kiss, he may be right and I wrong. It is not uncommon to see him greet a Christian brother with an old-fashioned hug and kiss. Some might list this as a fault, but if so, it cannot be too serious, and getting kissed by Brother Tom is like being caressed by all your godly ancestors at once.

I have also known Tom to fall asleep during some of his prolonged seasons of prayer. William T. MacAthur used to say that under certain circumstances the most religious thing a man could do was to go to sleep, and I have no doubt that Tom's occasional cat-nap while stretched before the Lord in the long night watches may be God's merciful provision for His servant's health. Once while trying to stay through an all-night season of prayer with him and a few others I learned by experience what such praying costs. Sometime after midnight I petered out and slipped off to my study for a snooze. At 8 o'clock the next morning I waked to hear Tom leaving the church. He had lasted out the night and I, though much younger than he, had surrendered to the sandman long before!

It is only fair to say, too, that Tom is sometimes capable of prejudice that is something less than scholarly. He insists, for instance, that the King James Version of the Scriptures is the only proper one for a Christian to read. "I know it is only a translation," he argues, "but God breathed on the translators as He did on no others, and thus preserved them from error. Of course," he adds meditatively, "they did call the Holy Spirit 'it' in the eighth chapter of Romans. But that was just a mistake." There you have it. The translators were divinely preserved from error, but they made a mistake! That comes perilously near to being an Irish bull, but if one is to be committed, who could better qualify for it than the man from County Antrim, Ireland?

Sometimes also Tom can become very much of a tease. He particularly loves to josh his American friends about the inferiority of all things American to everything Irish. After his accident at the hotel fire in Chicago I went to see him often. He lay cruelly crushed by the long fall to the concrete pavement. His hip and thigh were fractured, his back broken in several places and one of his hands burned severely. He lay in what must have been harsh, grinding pain. To afford what assurance I could, I bent close to his ear and told him that we had secured for him one of the best orthopedic surgeons obtainable. For all his great pain he managed a sly grin. "Ye mean he is one of the bust in Amurica," he whispered, "but don't forget, we have butter ones in Ireland."

Tom is not a finished speaker by any means, but in an average message he manages to throw off so many sparks of real inspiration that his hearers forget everything but the wonder of the truth he is proclaiming. His messages tend to be circular, that is, they travel around to the same thought again and again. He reminds me of the advice given to a young preacher to the effect that if he was going to harp on one string he should make that string a humdinger! Tom's string is love, fastened between the two pegs of faith and prayer. And that string is so long and so vibrant that it is seldom monotonous to listen to no matter how many times you hear it.

In my effort to escape the charge of writing an extravagant panegyric, I have combed through my knowledge of Tom Haire to try to find some flaw in his godly life. The fact that I could discover no more than is mentioned here is probably a finer commendation than the most eloquent eulogy could ever be.

## Praying with Understanding

Leonard Ravenhill, the English evangelist, opened a series of meetings in the church where I have been pastor for some years, and as usual brought along Tom Haire as a companion and prayer helper. The two men are as different as night and day, the evangelist being a veritable son of thunder and Tom a gentle, affectionate soul who will listen to anyone's troubles as long as necessary and permit himself to be taken advantage of without limit just to be sure he will not miss someone who may actually be in need of help. The fiery Englishman bears patiently with the slow, smiling Irishman. Each one makes up what the other lacks and together they make a remarkable team.

Tom had not been long among us till he began to sense the spiritual condition of the people. "The trouble I find here," he said after a while, "is not gross sin of a fleshly kind, but sin on a higher, spiritual level." And this "higher" kind of sin was to him very much more serious. Pride, self-confidence, refined unbelief, worldly mindedness—these are far more destructive and much harder to get at than those cruder sins which are the stock in trade of evangelistic preaching. Thereafter Tom's prayers followed very closely the direction indicated by the specific needs of the people. Tom doesn't like to waste prayer.

This habit of carefully surveying the situation before setting out to pray about things is characteristic of Tom Haire. To him prayer is a science whose laws can be learned. Praying itself is not a shot in the dark, not a net cast into the sea with the hope of a good catch. Praying is working along with God in the fulfillment of the divine plan. Praying is fighting close up at the front where the sharp deciding action is taking place.

According to Tom, there is such a thing as strategic prayer, that is, prayer that takes into account what the devil is trying to accomplish and where he is working and attacks him at that strategic point. "Don't waste your time praying around the edges," he says. "Go for the devil direct. Pray him lost from souls. Weaken his hold on people by direct attack. Then your prayers will count and the work of God will get done."

Tom makes much of the believer's authority in Christ. Over the protests of the cautious expositor, he appropriates Scripture that might be proved to belong to a future age. "God says we are kings and priests," he declares, "and what is a king without a kingdom? There is a sphere where we can have full dominion in prayer. Complete authority is ours. We only need to ask and we shall receive." If this were mere theory we might dismiss it as being simply an error in interpretation, but it has been proved in the fires of practical living. God has given to His praying servant great power to command, to demand, and the results have been and are many and unusual.

One lesson we may learn from this man is to pray intelligently and with planned direction. When he cannot find the will of God about a thing he is as helpless as any man, but once he knows what God wants him to ask in prayer his voice takes on bold assurance. A young doctor in our congregation became suddenly ill with an acute form of hepatitis. He was taking advanced work in a Chicago hospital before returning to Ethiopia for his second term as a missionary. We asked Tom to pray for him, and he prayed dutifully but without much assurance. "God has not told me what He wants to do," he repeated again and again. "I have not heard from God about this." Shortly thereafter the doctor lapsed into a coma and in a few days died, leaving a wife and child and an empty place on his mission field. No one could fathom the ways of God in it all, but it did not stagger Tom. God had operated after His own hidden purpose, and for this once He had withheld His secret from all of us. "All I know about it," said Tom, shaking his head solemnly, "is that God must have had some strong reason for wanting His servant with Him." Some of us who have lived close to this man believe that if God had wanted to keep the doctor here on earth He would have told Tom.

Like many another plain believer who has sat at the feet of Christ longer than he has sat before books on theology, Tom tends to great simplicity in everything. All those fine shadings of truth that slow down so many highly educated persons are lost on Tom. To him there are just two forces in the universe, God and Satan, and if a specific phenomenon does not originate with one it will be found to have originated with the other. That may be oversimplification, but it puts an edge on his ax and gets results.

For one who fights as many battles as does this Irishman, he is remarkably restful and self-possessed. Or better say, God-possessed, for his tranquility is not natural; it is a divine thing. One of his favorite words is "relax." He cannot see the good of tension anywhere. "Climb up into the arms of God," he says, "and relax. Getting things from God is as natural as breathing. When we pray we exhale; when we take the answer we inhale. Prayer is simply a restful inhaling and exhaling in the Spirit of God."

It is significant that Dr. A.B. Simpson in his day

taught the same truth in almost the same words. A stanza of one of his songs runs like this:

> *I am breathing out my longings*
> *In Thy listening, loving ears;*
> *I am breathing in Thy answers,*
> *Stilling every doubt and fear.*

This becomes all the more remarkable when it is remembered that Tom Haire never came under the influence of A.B. Simpson. He never heard him preach nor read one of his books. It can only be explained as the same Spirit saying the same thing to different men who listen to His voice with equal care.

## Praying in Tribulation

It was 4 o'clock on a bitterly cold November morning when the telephone rang and an excited voice told me that the Norwood Hotel was burning and the guests were fleeing into the street in their night clothes to escape the flames.

Leonard Ravenhill, the English evangelist, and his prayer helper, Tom Haire, who were engaged in evangelistic meetings in our local church, were staying at the Norwood. My informant could tell me nothing about these men. He only knew that some guests had died in the fire and others had been badly injured.

In a few minutes one of the elders of the church picked me up and together we raced over the icy streets to the scene of the fire. The police and firemen had the area blocked off. The basement of the First

45

Nazarene Church, located within one block of the hotel, had been converted into a first-aid station and the less seriously injured victims of the fire were being cared for there. A hurried search among the shivering and frightened persons who had gathered in the church basement failed to discover either Ravenhill or Haire. The excited guests could not tell us anything about them, but some thought that the two men had been among the victims who had jumped from the hotel windows.

The next logical place to look was St. Bernard Hospital, a few blocks away. There the scene was one of confusion. We stopped one of the hurrying sisters and inquired whether two Protestant evangelists had been admitted to the hospital in the last few minutes. The sister replied that she did not know. "But," she added, "as I helped to bring in one elderly man who had been hurt in the fire, he patted my cheek and asked me if I loved Jesus." We did not need to ask further. We had found Tom.

Both Mr. Ravenhill and Mr. Haire had been seriously injured by the long jump to the pavement from the third story window of the hotel. Both had broken bones in many parts of their bodies, Tom suffered deep burns on one hand and Ravenhill received internal injuries.

Nothing else within the sphere of my own experience has demonstrated so beautifully the real quality of present-day Christians as did the hotel accident suffered by the two evangelists. The news wires carried the story to every part of the United States and Canada and finally to England and Ireland. Immediately telegrams and long distance calls began to flood into my office from far parts of the continent. Churches wrote to offer assistance; Christian nurses and doctors volunteered their aid; visitors came in great numbers and prayer went up like incense from coast to coast. The two men hovered for a while between life and death and then slowly began to get well. Whatever cynical unbelief may say, there are many persons who believe that the multitude of intercessions made for others were returning on the heads of God's servants. For everyone who says, "Why did this happen to praying men?" there are others who exclaim, "How could mortal man come through all this and still live?" By every natural evidence they should have died. That they are alive today is due to the kindness of God and the determined prayers of God's people.

The weeks spent in St. Bernard Hospital revealed the workings of God in many ways. Since this sketch concerns Mr. Haire I shall focus attention upon him mainly, though it should be said also that some of the experiences of Evangelist Ravenhill were not less wonderful.

It was not long before the news had spread through the hospital that a Protestant "saint" had come among them. Nurses, doctors, supervisors and "sisters" of various kinds came to see Tom for themselves. Some of them admitted that they had not been aware that such men as Tom were still to be found running loose. Though their teachings forbade them to believe that Tom was a real Christian, their yearning hearts were better and more charitable than their dogmas, and they soon accepted him not as a Christian only but as a superior saint who could teach them the things of the Spirit.

Among those who visited Tom was a distinguished professor of philosophy at University of Notre Dame. He came not to try to convert Tom but to hear from his mouth the wonders of a life of prayer and worship. In the course of his conversations he admitted that he was very much dissatisfied with the kind of Christian being produced within the Catholic fold. "They come to me and confess their sins," he said, "and then go back and do the same things again. I do not believe in that kind of religion. When a man comes to Christ he should come with John the Baptist repentance." This may sound trite to the average evangelical, but coming from a highly placed prelate of the Roman Catholic Church it is little less than astounding. And the whole experience suggests that there may be many others enmeshed in the toils of Romanism who would look our way if we presented more examples of true godliness to catch their attention.

Tom's experience in the hospital was not without humorous incidents, though Tom was extremely careful never to give offense to the Catholic personnel. One Friday he suddenly developed an appetite for meat and called a nurse to him. "I say, suster," he began, "I crave a wee piece o' roast chucken. D'ye suppose ye cud get me some?" The nurse said no. It was Friday, and besides, chicken was not served to patients in that hospital. That was final. But Tom persisted. "But, suster. Ye don't know who I am! Tomorrah the British consul is comin' to see me. And besides that, look at the green light above me bed, put there in honor of auld Ireland. Now do I get some chucken?" Tom's blue eyes were twinkling. The consul's visit was scarcely to be in honor of Tom, and the green light above the bed surely had no remote relation to Tom's birthplace. The nurse left the room shaking her head doubtfully. After a while she reappeared all smiles, and on a tray she carried a plate laden with roast chicken. Tom ate the meal with relish. He undoubtedly enjoyed it, but more than all he enjoyed the fact that he had gotten roast chicken in a Catholic hospital on Friday.

One day as a supervisor was in his room, Tom suddenly asked her to pray for him. She promised she would go immediately to the chapel and say a prayer for him. But that would not do. "No," Tom insisted, "I want you to pray for me now. Right here." The surprised sister scrambled around in her voluminous bag and came up with a prayer book out of which she read a prayer. Then to be sure she would not leave, Tom grabbed her hand and hung on. "Now, suster, I'll pray for you." Then he launched into one of his tender, impassioned prayers while the sister stood reverently with bowed head. When he was through there was awe in her voice as she said, "That wasn't a memorized prayer, was it, Tom? That came right out of your heart. The Holy Ghost must have given you that." Until the day breaks and the shadows flee away it will not be revealed how much was accomplished through the suffering man of God by such faithful witnessing among persons who for all their blindness are at least reverent and serious-minded.

When the men were recovered sufficiently to be moved, a United States Army ambulance plane flew them to New York where they were the guests of the army for one day. Then they were flown overseas to their respective homes in England and Ireland.

In a few months, much improved physically, Tom came back to the United States. When all financial matters had been adjusted and the time was ripe to settle his accounts, Tom called on his doctor to pay the bill. The doctor looked him over and waited to hear what he would say. He had been told that he could expect a request for a discount. He was definitely not prepared for what he was to hear.

"Now, Doctor," Tom began "I want to settle up with you. I understand that you expect me to ask for a discount on my bill on the grounds that I am a Christian worker. But, Doctor, I shall do nothing of the kind. You see, I am connected with the Deity and I run my business on the same principles as God runs His. God never asks for discounts. His method is to give full measure, pressed down, shaken together and running over. And I want to do the same. Here is a signed check made out to you. Only the amount is left blank. Now you take it, write in any amount you please and it will be honored, and I'd rather you made it too much than too little."

This was more than the Catholic surgeon could stand. He broke down and wept, threw his arms around Tom and kissed him like a son. "I have never seen a Christian like you before in all my life, Tom. Here, hand me the check." Then he deducted $250 from the total bill and wrote in the reduced amount.

While Tom was going through the long siege of suffering after his accident he was forced for the first time in years to give up his habit of praying three nights each week. He missed having these long seasons of intercession, but he did not let it bother him nor did he allow himself to get under bondage because he could not pray as before. God knew that His servant would be back at his regular habit as soon as he could, and Tom knew that He knew and understood. Between friends there are some things that can be taken for granted.

One day not long ago Tom came shuffling into the church, his face shining a bit more than usual and his voice full of excitement like a boy that had just received a sled or a pony for his birthday. The reason for his new joy was that God had enabled him to go back to his old habit of all-night prayer again! He feels so much "butter," he says, that he can stay up all night now without any trouble.

But Tom will probably never again be able to kneel before God as he had been doing for fifty years. The crushed pelvis and the broken back are "butter," it is true, but they will not permit him to bend very much at best. He must now do his praying sitting up for the most part, though when he is by himself he often stretches full length on the floor as he goes over his long prayer lists or worships the Lord in the beauty of holiness. I have come upon him sometimes lying prone before the Lord quietly wrestling against the evil one whom he calls "Seten." So completely free is he that when he is interrupted in prayer by the unexpected entrance of a friend, he simply breaks off his praying, scrambles to his feet and enters into a relaxed and delightful conversation about anything that the visitor may have on his mind. Tom will talk about anything, but he is never so keen nor so original as when talking about the goodness of God and the power of prayer.

The doctors have told Tom that his accident has probably prolonged his life many years by forcing a long rest just at the period in his life when his heart stood in need of it. Of course such a matter is in the hand of God and any prediction of longevity would be altogether rash and foolhardy. But one thing is sure: Whether he stays among us for many years or slips off to heaven tomorrow is not of any consequence to Tom. He lived so long on the portico of heaven that he will feel quite at home when the Father comes out and invites him inside.

## The Secret of Successful Praying

As never before I feel the great need for intense research into the deeper mysteries of prayer.

I see on the distant horizon truth, which, if I can attain to through grace, should to some degree shake hell and retard its outpourings into the world and the Church in our day. This truth lies mainly in John 17 (verses 21-23):

That they all may be one; as thou, Father, art in me, and I in thee, that they also may be one in us: that the world may believe that thou hast sent me. And the glory which thou gavest me I have given them; that they may be one, even as we are one: I in them, and thou in me, that they may be made perfect in one; and that the world may know that thou hast sent me, and hast loved them, as thou has loved me.

The *purpose* that lies in this passage, as I see it, is that the world may come to believe in Christ. The *condition* is that we believers grow more perfectly into harmony with and correspondence to the Deity. This is a restoration to that state enjoyed by our first parents before the Fall. It is described by the words, "So God created man in his own image, in the image of God created he him" (Genesis 1:27). In the next sentence God said, "Have dominion." Those who are in the divine image have divine authorization to subdue the earth. The means by which this authority is exercised is prayer.

The first Adam failed. He was but a creature of God. The new creation which is brought into being through the work of Christ in atonement is *born* of God and receives His true nature, so that the fullness of the Godhead indwells the human personality. This is a distinct advance over the position enjoyed by the first Adam. The human personality becomes the outward instrument of the Almighty Inworker. If this becomes true in actual experience, then the "subduing" and the "dominion" should be made factual in the earth wherever our prayer rights are exercised in faith.

That a Spirit-led Christian can actually do the very work of Christ is plainly taught in the Scriptures. Paul said, "To me to live is Christ" (Philippians 1:21). John said, "As he is, so are we in this world" (1 John 4:17) And I think we have hardly yet dared to face the mighty implications in the words of our Lord in John 14:12: "Verily, verily, I say unto you, he that believeth on me, the works that I do shall he do also; and greater works than these shall he do; because I go unto my Father."

Sometimes I imagine I am a bottle filled to the utmost; then I think I am that bottle in the middle of the waters before the firmament was created or the dry land appeared, with infinite miles of grace beneath me and around me in all directions. The little bottle doubts sometimes through the suggestions of the serpent. Will there be enough water to keep it filled and to float it safely forever? But the doubts are only for a moment. Thank God there is always enough in Christ!

As in the Garden there was a serpent, so now there are serpents to tempt God's redeemed people. Only now the dark serpents have been joined by white ones. The dark ones are on Skid Row and are terrible because of their frightful physical manifestations such as drinking, dope addiction and other such gross sins. The white ones are of the same nature as the others, but are illuminated by the "the angel of light" who transforms them into white ones with supernatural power to work in human personalities. These may lead people to speak with the tongues of angels, foretell the future, understand all mysteries and be driven with a passionate desire for the attainment of all knowledge.

Our colleges, sad to think, are alive with white serpents, moving men to seek honor among men, such honor as superior learning brings. It is difficult to get prayer into its primary place in our colleges, even in our Christian colleges. The head, the voice, the dress, the gestures—these take first place and are eagerly cultivated. But we can never cast out devils with the intellect, however cultured. Even casting out devils may be counterfeited by the devil, who will withdraw his power for a moment to deceive the unwary. Casting out devils, speaking wonderful words or moving mountains may be no evidence at all of true Christianity.

> Many will say to me in that day, Lord, Lord, have we not prophesied in thy name? and in thy name have cast out devils? and in thy name done many wonderful works? And then will I profess unto them, I never knew you; depart from me, ye that work iniquity. (Matthew 7:22-23)

Martyrdom without love will prove to be a snare. Giving my body to be burned or starving it by fasting is in direct violation of the command of God in creation. "Give ye them to eat" is in harmony with the purpose of God, for He made many things to be used for food for mankind. True fasting is the result of spiritual preoccupation, as when Moses went into the mount and continued without food for forty days. He did not need food then, for he was seeing God's face. The sins of Aaron and the people of Israel lay heavily on his heart and crowded out the desire for food. He spent his days in intercession. I think he saw by faith the Lamb slain before the foundation of the world, and as he moved into spiritual union with the Lamb he was enabled to intercede successfully for Israel. God answered with the most wonderful words ever spoken to man: "I have pardoned according to thy word" (Numbers 14:20). Moses was offered the opportunity to become greater than the sinning multitude, but in declining this offer and identifying himself with Israel he came into spiritual harmony with the Lamb who was later to give His life for His sinning friends. Is this what Paul meant when he expressed a desire to be "made conformable" unto His death?

Fasting and faith are to be secondary always. Perhaps I should say, conscious faith and purposive fasting. We are commanded to "have the faith of God." This is a result of a loving understanding of the mind of God and comes as He sits beside the refining vessel and skins off the dross from our natures. Then we see His face and understand the effort. God thus gives the gift of affinity. It is a kind of spiritual birth within us and is accompanied by love. God is love and without love everything else is vain.

It is impossible to overemphasize the importance of love in the Christian life. Though I have all faith and have not love I am as salt that has lost its savor. Love cannot sin, for God is love and God can never sin. Love is a fire that consumes sin. The Church clamors for mountain-removing faith and meritorious praying and fasting, but if all this is secretly to be used to attain fame among the saints then it is inspired by the white serpent. Christ prayed all night because He was drawn irresistibly to it as by a magnet within Him. It was the result of an irresistible urge rather than of conscious purpose. He that saith he abideth in Him ought to walk even as He walked—and prayed. The same motives that governed Him should govern us.

The secret power of prayer is affinity with Christ and conformity to His image. The urge to pray must come from God and not from our own ambition. Increasing measure of Christlikeness will mean increased power in prayer. Then when He shall appear, we shall be like Him, for we shall see Him as He is.

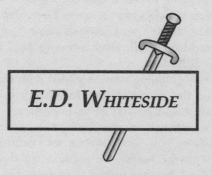

# 3

# The Praying Man of Pittsburgh

*E.D. Whiteside, known as "the Praying Man of Pittsburgh," would often find solutions to problems with, "Brethren, let us pray." He ministered in slums and prisons for much of his life, and it was said that he had more friends among the bums of Pittsburgh than any other man. A year before he died, Whiteside said, "I desire to live that I may pray. I do not want to go to heaven yet. I want to stay a while longer to pray."*

*Edited and condensed from* The Life of E.D. Whiteside: The Praying Man of Pittsburgh *by E.R. Carner, now out of print.*

To be with E.D. Whiteside was to have a sense of the divine presence; to pray with him was to be led into the Holy of Holies. He was a saint in the deepest sense of the word.

For some fifteen years it was my privilege to work with him in the annual Pittsburgh Bible and missionary convention. I looked forward to those visits with the keenest anticipation—nor was I ever disappointed. I can see those great crowds now, gathered in Carnegie Music Hall, from morning until night, for seven or eight days.

The very building seemed gilded with the glory of God, and the power of the Holy Spirit rested upon the weakest and poorest of us preachers. I think the people sometimes wondered why the presence of the Lord was so real. But some of us knew the secret. While we were before the public, that dear faithful man of God, his face turned to heaven, was interceding for hours at a time.

W.P. Philpott, pastor
Moody Memorial Church, Chicago, IL


E.D. Whiteside was indeed a spiritual father as he visited in the hundreds of homes throughout his extensive parish. Well do I remember the day he visited our home at a time of great need and discouragement. One of my sisters was very low with severe spinal disease. Not for weeks had she stood on her feet. The slightest noise or disturbance seemed to her unbearable.

Mr. Whiteside quietly knelt in prayer at the bedside. According to the Word of God he anointed my sister with oil and offered the prayer of faith. In a short time my sister was walking through the house praising God. What a pall lifted from our home that day!

J.D. Williams, director of education<br>The Christian and Missionary Alliance

With several others I was at the altar seeking to be filled with the Holy Spirit. E.D. Whiteside knelt beside me as I prayed and waited.

"Has He come?" Mr. Whiteside asked.

"I think so," I replied.

"That will not do," he answered.

I saw his meaning. "Then, yes, I take Him at His Word. I have put all on the altar unreservedly. I will believe His promise to come in and abide!"

I went on reckoning the transaction done. The Bible became a new Book. Its promises seemed literally to stand out on the pages. . . . I received new faith. . . . I had strength almost unlimited for teaching, caring for the sick or dying, and many kinds of Christian service. I praise God for those like Mr. Whiteside, who know the way and can help others to find God.

Mrs. E. J. Calvert<br>Oil City, PA

E.D. Whiteside was a faithful pastor. I have known him to travel long distances to make one pastoral call, and he did not go by automobile. Once Christian and Missionary Alliance ministers in western Pennsylvania were holding their monthly session of prayer in a town distant from Pittsburgh. At the lunch hour Mr.

Whiteside was missing. No one seemed to know where he was. It turned out he had gone to call on someone in need. He did not go during the morning prayer time nor in the afternoon when, again, there was a prayer service. He chose the lunch hour in which to minister in prayer and fellowship to one in need.

Arthur Petrie, minister, writer
Pittsburgh, PA

In 1913 I became the pastor of Central Christian Church in Pittsburgh. Proximity enabled me frequently to come in touch with Mr. Whiteside, both in his church and in the home he operated at 320 Cedar Avenue. I always left him feeling that I had been in the presence of a priest of God.

John H. Cable, principal
The Missionary Training Institute,
Nyack, NY

Once when I was passing through Pittsburgh, I stopped off to see E.D. Whiteside. By then he was in his sixties. He insisted on carrying my handbag all the way to Union Station. When he learned that I intended to ride the day coach that night, he quickly slipped over to the ticket window and purchased a Pullman berth for me. I protested when he handed me the ticket, but he would not hear of it.

"You need rest," he said. E.D. Whiteside never thought of himself.

William Christie
pioneer missionary to Tibet

Who was this "praying man of Pittsburgh" whose life influenced so many so positively? Who was this humble saint whose funeral, held in Pittsburgh's famed Carnegie Music Hall, drew preachers, teachers, mission workers, evangelists and overseas missionaries, as well as devoted rank-and-file people of the area—the largest funeral the undertaker had ever seen?

This truly humble and selfless man, always hiding behind the Lord Jesus Christ and keeping his own name and presence in the background, deserves a closer look by all who want to know God. Not that Edward Drury Whiteside would himself want such attention. Rather, it is so that further glory might go to the Lord Jesus, the Secret of Whiteside's lastingly beautiful life, the secret of every lastingly beautiful life. Whiteside was, in experience, crucified with Christ. He lived by the faith of the Son of God who loved him and gave Himself for him. Like the first followers of our Lord, he lived so in God's presence that people noted he had been with Jesus.

Here is his story.

## A Godly Heritage

E.D. Whiteside did not plan for a biography. To have done so would not have been consistent with his life, so free from thoughts of self. We are left, therefore, with but fragments of information about his early past. But such fragments as we have are cross-sections of a tree both sturdy and healthy.

Whiteside's maternal grandfather, Joseph Barlow,

was born into a well-to-do colonial family living in Amboy, New Jersey. Eight years later his maternal grandmother, Martha Wright, was a Valentine's Day gift to her parents, whose estate adjoined the Vanderbilts' on Staten Island. Both ancestors, therefore, would have been children while the Revolutionary War was in progress. The loyalties of these two families were to the British crown. After the American victory, they with others emigrated in 1784 to Canada, settling in St. John, New Brunswick. In 1788, Joseph Barlow and Martha Wright married. Their ninth child, Martha, born eighteen years later in 1806, would one day be Edward Whiteside's mother.

## Godly Parentage . . .

Excerpts from an 1876 letter seventy-year-old Martha Barlow Whiteside wrote to her grown son Edward succinctly reveal the godly character of this woman:

[Christ Jesus] is my Refuge and Savior, my All in all. He has His everlasting arms under and round about me. His presence is with me always. He has spared me many years. From my youth up He has watched over me. When I look back I see many dangers I have been kept from. I know I could not have escaped in my own strength.

When I was a young child, my mother opened our home to a weekly prayer meeting. At one of those meetings the pastor and several of the others put their hands on my head and said, "Won't you give your heart to God?" Then and there I decided to serve the Lord. It was many years after that before I really did so, and, oh, how many temptations I have been subject to! I know it was the Lord Jesus who was watching over me, restraining me.

I cannot tell you the time or the place when the change occurred, but I knew it had happened, for all was changed and everything had become new.

After I was converted, I had a time with the devil. One night I went to prayer meeting very happy. But I was no sooner seated than Satan was there to plague me:

"You think you are a Christian," Satan said, "but you are not. If you were, you could tell the place and the time you were saved. You are just deceiving yourself and others. Everyone in this room knows you are a deceiver and a hypocrite."

As soon as the meeting closed I hurried home. *I must settle this before I sleep tonight,* I said to myself. I ran up to my room and knelt down before God. I was not on my knees two minutes before I heard a voice saying, "Daughter, your sins are all forgiven you!" I looked up and the room was lit with the most beautiful light I had ever seen or ever will see until I get where there is no darkness. From that day to this, I have never had a doubt that I am fully the

Lord's. A thousand devils could not make me believe otherwise! Has not God been good to me? I shall praise Him when I get home. I am longing to go!

Your loving
Mother

Actually, Edward's mother lived nearly a score more years. When the end came in February, 1893, it was peaceful.

## ... and Meticulous Discipline

Martha Whiteside was as meticulous in raising her children as she was in making sure her salvation. When Edward needed discipline, his mother herself administered the biblical "rod of correction," and followed it by prayer.

"I could stand the whippings my mother gave me," Whiteside long afterward would recall with a smile of loving memory, "but I could not stand her prayers."

Edward's father, Henry Whiteside, arrived in Saint John from England while still a young man. In due course he met and fell in love with Martha Barlow, and the two were married. For fifty years he was a customs official in St. John. Over time he became one of the city's leading citizens. He was also an official in the old Centenary Methodist Church in the city.

"His name was a synonym for uprightness, honor, integrity and true Christianity," commented one who knew him.

In 1877 a great fire swept St. John, almost destroying the entire town. In the flames of that conflagration both the Whiteside home and their beloved church home were consumed. Henry moved to Sussex, Nova Scotia but died within a year or two.

Much later, after the home going of their mother, Henry Whiteside, Jr. commented in a letter to his brother Edward: "I thank God for our lineage. Seldom on both sides of the house does one find so many persons of honorable character, made so by the righteousness of Jesus Christ."

## "Five Noble Boys"

Edward Drury Whiteside was born in St. John in 1848, the fourth of "five noble boys"—Charles, Henry, Frederic, Edward and Arthur. (Two sisters died while still very young.) The Christian influence of these five sons of Henry and Martha Whiteside would extend far beyond the St. John community where they were reared. Both Edward and Arthur were chosen of the Lord for the work of the ministry. For a time Arthur was a missionary to the Oka Indians on the far frontier of Canada. Later he worked among the hardy frontier people of Saskatchewan, then in the towns of that province and still later in his native New Brunswick.

We do not know exactly when or where E.D. Whiteside responded to the Lord's voice and put his faith in Christ's atoning work. We do know it was during a revival meeting, possibly in Montreal. A deacon knelt beside him and tried to help. But this young man of sturdy, straight up-and-down honesty would not say he had met God until he was certain. So the deacon left, and Edward continued to pray. Presently he leaped to his feet with a shout, exclaiming, "I've got it!"

Later he would correct the statement, changing the "it" to "Him"—Christ Jesus. But the fact was indisputable. The great transaction had taken place. Jesus was Lord in Edward Whiteside's life.

## A Frustrated Preacher Finds Healing

If not at the time of his conversion, then shortly thereafter, God called E.D. Whiteside to the ministry. As a boy he had attended the public schools of St. John and later the University of New Brunswick. Because all his family members were Methodists, it was natural that he should choose Methodist-related Allison College for his seminary training. Upon graduation he joined the Methodist Episcopal conference of New Brunswick. The conference appointed him to Charlottetown, Prince Edward Island.

Whiteside's ministry at Charlottetown was cut short by what were probably attacks of gallstones, a malady that had pursued him since he was a child. The attacks became frequent, compelling him to resign from the ministry. But not before a godly woman in his congregation shared with him a written account of the physical healing of Miss Jennie Smith, a Maryland railway evangelist. In direct answer to prayer, God had marvelously healed this woman of paralysis, at the same time supplying her temporal needs. As the suffering Whiteside read this record, the Holy Spirit seemed to whisper to him, *I will do the same for you if you will trust Me absolutely.*

The conservative and proper Whiteside was not yet ready for so radical a step. "Since that implied a life of faith on every line," he commented many years later, "it seemed like a big undertaking. I did not promptly launch out on God. Instead, I sought more light on divine healing."

Whiteside allowed the noted Dr. Charles Cullis, Boston physician and Episcopal layman, to anoint him with oil and pray for him. Whiteside remained unimproved.

## Eleven Years of Drifting

He decided to give up the ministry permanently. He turned to farming, hoping the fresh air and sunshine would effect a cure. "But God did not allow sunshine and air to do the work He had designed to do Himself," Whiteside said.

For eleven years—1877 to 1888—Whiteside "roamed around, . . . seeking health and not finding it." He needed a livelihood. He tried to get into business. He failed at every turn. Through it all, he sought to serve the Lord. And very tenderly the Lord watched over him. God was waiting for this servant of His to quit trying in his own strength to be healed and begin to trust the Healer.

In one very important matter, those eleven years were *not* wasted. Whiteside found a wife who was the woman of God's own choosing for him. Annie Hagarty came from a long line of staunch Irish Protestants. From her early years she was a devout person of the highest Christian character. After their marriage, the couple plunged into church work first at Sussex, then at St. John, Edward doing as much as his poor health allowed.

Suspecting the rigorous Canadian winters were detrimental, Edward and Annie Whiteside moved to Connecticut, taking work with the Connecticut Bible Society. But poor health continued to pursue Edward.

Whiteside heard of a New York City minister, Rev. Albert B. Simpson, who believed that the Lord Jesus healed the sick in answer to the prayer of faith. He decided to investigate. The year was 1886.

"I was skeptical," Whiteside wrote some thirty years later. "But pressed by my desperate condition, I went to New York and found the Oberamergau Theater on Twenty-third Street, where Mr. Simpson then was holding his meetings. I sat at a good vantage point to scan the situation. Being in mental and physical despondency, I was not reassured as I watched the people entering the hall. Should I stay or flee?

"Presently a noble-looking man walked up the center aisle, knelt at the front in silent prayer and then stood to announce the opening hymn. I surmised the man to be Simpson. At the same time I sensed a Presence more real than that of Mr. Simpson or any other person. The Lord Jesus was there in that place. I sat subdued and awed.

"The brief address by Mr. Simpson and the bright testimonies that followed made Jesus ever more consciously real. At the close of the testimonies, I arose and said, 'I came here broken down in health. Being despondent, I cruelly criticized in my mind all I saw. I am changed chiefly because of the humble, Christlike spirit evidenced by the leader and everyone who has taken part. I have been made to feel that you possess what I lack and must have.'

"At the conclusion of the meeting Mr. Simpson seized my hand and invited me to visit him and to remain a few days. I did so, and when I returned to my home it was with a new vision of Christ and His sufficiency. I had a new, overwhelming sense of God's grace. The future was bright with the prospect of victory. That vision began the end of my dark despair and physical collapse."

## Healed in Pittsburgh

Shortly after his visit with A.B. Simpson, Whiteside accepted a job offer in Pittsburgh. Ten years of "roaming" had gone by. He was still in no better health. As the couple stepped off the train in Pittsburgh, the Lord had news for E.D. Whiteside. Here is how he told it.

"The Lord said to me, 'I brought you to Pittsburgh to establish a slum mission here.' I thought I had brought myself to Pittsburgh, and as to the slum mission, I said nothing to anyone because I thought I was not fit for that kind of work. I started in the insurance business."

But Whiteside and his wife also plunged into a year of strenuous city missionary work. That first year he made 5,129 home visits in Pittsburgh, an average of fourteen calls a day! And all the time he was desperately ill. He was becoming increasingly helpless.

It then had been eleven years since ill health forced him to abandon his Methodist pastorate in Charlottetown. For eleven years he had searched for health. He had farmed. He had pursued other occupations. Always he was as active as he could be in the work of the Lord. For all of those years he had been aware that God supernaturally heals the sick in answer to believing prayer. He had read the testimony of Jennie Smith, the railroad evangelist. He had been anointed and prayed for by Dr. Charles Cullis. He had listened to A.B. Simpson and witnessed his healing ministry. Now, a year after his arrival in Pittsburgh, he finally was ready to "throw up his hands" in surrender.

"Did you ever 'throw up your hands'?" Whiteside asked in a letter he wrote many years later to his younger brother Arthur, reflecting on the spiritual transaction that marked his life. He continued:

> In vain I sought and prayed and traveled back and forth. I consumed years in the search for health. But I finally "threw up my hands." That was what I needed to do. That is what is always needed—if the sinner would get saved, or the believer get sanctified, or the sick one get healed by God.
>
> To my utter amazement, when I finally threw up my hands, Jesus instantly touched me. His divine life flowed through my body. It

was a shock—sudden, unexpected, startling. He touched me when I threw up my hands, broken up in despair. Everything around me had suddenly grown dark as midnight. The presence of a host of demons and the awful reality of a yawning hell were all that I was conscious of. As I sank to my knees in my room that early morning, I threw up my hands without taking time to reason or frame a prayer. I could only utter this cry of hopeless, helpless surrender: "O God, help me!"

Then like a flash of electricity it happened. Every part of my body and every nerve fibre were controlled by a strange sensation. The sensation intensified, bowing me lower and lower to the floor. I was filled with ecstatic bliss. My physical frame seemed unable to stand the strain. A moment before, I was sinking into hell. Now I was in danger of dying from overjoy!

"What's the matter?" Annie, who had arisen, asked. She could see the glow on my face.

"I am healed! I am healed!" I exclaimed. Annie threw her arms around me and we laughed together, unable to control our joy.

## A Sea Change Experience

In terms of its effect on the years that followed, Whiteside's physical healing was probably the most momentous crisis of his life. His faith now grew exceedingly. Nothing seemed to daunt him. He had learned in this one great experience to trust God.

It was a ready formula for the thousands of other crises that would follow. He had died a deep death to self-will and unbelief of every kind, and the resurrection side of that death was proportionately glorious and beautiful.

"Why did it not occur sooner?" Whiteside asks. "Why did it not occur in Charlottetown? I believe God would have done so if I had 'thrown up my hands.' I had a strong will, and it hindered me. It was quite natural for me to imagine I would get healed if only I persevered and refused to give in. It was conceit to imagine I could get healed by piety, prayer or perseverance. When I became so helpless I could not even try to believe or frame a prayer, when perseverance was at an end, *then* the Lord healed me. He spoke to me that instant and said, 'This is the first time you trusted Me.'

"It was deeply humiliating to be told it was 'the first time.' For years friends had commended me for my faith. 'Oh, you have great faith!' 'I wish I had your faith, Brother Whiteside.' But God knew better. I could have had healing and been a help to countless others if I had known it was God's will to heal His children. There was no teaching, no preaching, there were no testimonies to that end, and here the Bible is full of it. It is so simple, so Christlike, so honoring to God, so magnifying to the atonement of Jesus."

## Prayer Builds a Ministry

Not long after God healed Whiteside, a woman approached him about beginning a mission to Pittsburgh's derelicts. The Moorehead building on Grant Street was available. She would pay the rent if he would trust the Lord for his own support and the mission's operating expenses.

"I had a hard struggle," Whiteside recalled. "I felt I was too little for so large an undertaking. But as I waited on the Lord, He gave me the verse, 'One man of you shall chase a thousand' (Joshua 23:10). God reminded me that I would have to stay little if I expected His help. There was also the matter of finances. Where would the money come from? God gave my wife the verse, 'My God shall supply all your need according to his riches in glory by Christ Jesus' (Philippians 4:19). So we started.

"We lived in one room above the mission hall, with a lodge room over us. There was plenty of noise and there was plenty of smoke. All of the five years we were in that room, our bed was too short for me. Had I complained, we would have received another, but the Lord permitted us to say nothing about it.

"The Lord told me to visit the local jail. I went. When I got there, the warden asked me what I wanted. I said, 'The Lord sent me to visit the jail.'

" 'That's against the rules,' the warden replied. 'You must see the commissioner.' But then he got nervous and unlatched the door. When I put my foot in, he changed his mind. 'This is against the rules,' he repeated. I said nothing—I was inside.

"The next time I went to the jail, the warden came to me. 'Mr. Whiteside,' he said, 'would you also come here and visit the prisoners at night? You may go anywhere.'

## The Penitentiary, Too

"Afterward, I went to the penitentiary. The officials discussed whether they should let me minister there. One man said, 'You had better not interfere with Mr. Whiteside. He has a higher Power back of him than the authorities of this penitentiary.' "

Whiteside's was the first such mission in Pittsburgh. For five years he labored day and night among the outcasts of the city. A contemporary describes his work:

> All classes came to that place. He would kneel down beside a dying young woman who had spent her life in sin and whisper, "The blood of Jesus Christ his Son cleanseth us from all sin" (1 John 1:7). He would take her by the hand as if she were his own daughter, and never let go until he had confidence in his own heart that her soul had found the shelter of Christ's blood.
>
> He went to the jail, from cage to cage, and always had a message of hope for the poor, unfortunate man. He paid special attention to those who had the sentence of death upon them. When one doomed to die confessed Christ, he would obtain permission to serve him Communion. His ministry was to build up heaven. . . . He did not look for popularity, but wanted to please God above all else.

## New Responsibilities

After five years' experience in what was largely a ministry to the outcasts of Pittsburgh, the Lord opened to Edward and Annie Whiteside a wider field. In brief, A.B. Simpson had come to Pittsburgh to establish a so-called branch of The Christian and Missionary Alliance. A week-long Bible and missionary conference, for which Simpson had engaged Carnegie Music Hall, would kick off the endeavor. Out of the concentrated week of meetings, Simpson hoped to see a permanent branch of his international missionary endeavor. And who better to superintend it than E.D. Whiteside?

"I had already been graciously helped in my spiritual life through Brother Simpson and the Alliance," Whiteside reflected years later. "Now he wanted to make our mission the nucleus of an Alliance branch, with me as the superintendent. 'Don't make me the superintendent,' I nervously exclaimed. 'Elect some other person and I will run errands for him.'

"My outburst was taken as an attempt at mirth, and the audience laughed. But I was downright in earnest. I turned to God in prayer. Urgently, audibly I said, 'O Lord, I appoint You as superintendent of the Pittsburgh branch of the Alliance. And I will run errands for You!' That moment I had wonderful relief in my soul and have had it ever since. God is still the Superintendent, in fact and reality, for to this day I recognize Him as such."

For thirty-two years Whiteside walked with God in

this new work. He saw it grow under God's blessing from the little nucleus centered in his slum mission to nearly a score of other centers in Pittsburgh and surrounding communities. As he lifted his eyes to the harvest, Whiteside saw, step-by-step, his role in reaping it. God Himself financed each new enterprise in answer to the faith of His servant. For example, God supplied tents for tent campaigns in various parts of the city and its suburbs. In these campaigns He saved people from their sins, He filled them with His Spirit, He healed them of physical disease and infirmity. Soon a like-minded company of people were ready to begin a church. One by one, faithful leaders would step up to carry the burden of that particular branch.

Whiteside was ever picking workers and praying them into the harvest fields. He did not try to hold them for himself. He got God's mind concerning them and then sent them forth.

## Godly Counselor

Whiteside had time for the questions of people, and these individuals in turn accepted his godly counsel. A mother asked his advice about sending her daughter to a prestigious high school in the city. "That's a wicked place," was his only comment. The woman investigated and discovered that what he had said was true. She enrolled her daughter elsewhere in high school.

On his way to conduct a service, Whiteside met a young woman for whom he had been praying. She was on her way to the same service. Discovering, as he suspected, that she was not living fully for Jesus, he urged her to surrender her life to God. She did so, soon entered college to train for missionary service and eventually went to China as a missionary.

As the reputation of this godly, humble man grew, he was sought after by the Lord's servants near and far. Maurice Ruben, who founded a mission to his fellow Jews in Pittsburgh, invited Whiteside to be on his board. He also worked closely with Peter Robinson, a noted black preacher in Pittsburgh. These three sat often together on the rostrum of Carnegie Music Hall in the days of Whiteside's great conventions. They beautifully exemplified the power of Christ's love to gather one church out of all the branches of the human race.

In his seventies, Whiteside looked back on his Pittsburgh ministry with these words:

> The whole secret of God's blessing these thirty-two years in Pittsburgh is this: I have of necessity consulted God in all things with deep humility and submission. *God* established over a dozen flourishing congregations in this city by causing me to trust Him for evangelists, open doors, tents, cottage meetings and expenses. When our mission became overcrowded, He prompted me to purchase property and build a church although there was no money in hand. Today the building is without encumbrance—a very valuable property.

God is faithful. He has never failed us. As Moses beautifully and strikingly said, "[The LORD] is . . . the faithful God, which keepeth covenant and mercy with them that love him and keep his commandments to a thousand generations" (Deuteronomy 7:9).

## The Home of Peace

Soon after Edward and Annie Whiteside assumed church responsibilities in Pittsburgh, God made it clear to them that they should establish a home in the city that would be open to every seeker after God. The Whitesides had no children of their own; consequently they could give full time to God's great family. All who knew them gladly testify that they measured up to that grand design. The Whitesides gave the great, full wealth of their hearts to all—adults and children—who had need of their ministry.

In turn, the Whitesides became spiritual "parents" to many of God's children. Generations knew this devoted couple as simply Daddy and Mother Whiteside.

With the same daring faith that characterized all of his ministry, Whiteside and his wife opened a home at 940 Penn Avenue in the heart of Pittsburgh. Downtown rent was high, but the Whitesides reasoned that a home of this character needed to be readily accessible from all points of the city. As the years went by, "Mr. Whiteside's Home," wherever it was, became to many a synonym for *blessing*.

## The Home

Penn Avenue between Ninth and Tenth Streets was a bustling, noisy thoroughfare. From early morning until late at night, street cars rumbled, trucks and drays clattered, the iron-shod hoofs of horses pounded on the pavement stones. Later came the motor cars, less noisy but swifter—indicative of the fevered hurry of city life. But within the portals of 940 Penn Avenue, there was tranquility.

We follow as a man—a visitor—mounts the steps to the front door. A neatly lettered sign, gilt on black, at the side of the entry announces the various public meetings of the week, for the home includes a small chapel. For the reassurance of any who are looking specifically for Mr. Whiteside, his name is also on the sign.

The visitor presses the electric push button beside the door to announce his presence. Soon the latch clicks and the door swings open. The visitor may find himself face-to-face with Whiteside or Mrs. Whiteside or one of the faithful associates living in the home. Whoever answers, he can be sure of a smile of welcome and an invitation to enter.

## The Man

If perchance it is Daddy Whiteside himself who answers, the visitor will hear a hearty "Good morning!" or "Good afternoon!" with never a trace of annoyance, no matter what task Whiteside has been taken from, no matter how many callers he had already greeted

81

that day, no matter how much a stranger this caller happens to be. Whiteside extends a hand of welcome, then conducts the visitor through the hallway to a quiet reception room, inviting him to be seated. The visitor senses the restfulness that pervades the home. The peace of God permeates it.

Whiteside is a man of medium height, slender of build. His eyes are gray-blue, his mouth is firm. He has the manner of one who never talks to fill time. He waits for the caller to state his errand. And if the caller has come with a problem or a burden, Whiteside makes him feel instinctively that he is face-to-face with a man he can trust, a man who can help.

The visitor has Whiteside's undivided attention as he shares his concern. The man of God says little, occasionally nodding his head in assent or adding a quiet "Yes." When the caller has unburdened his heart, Daddy Whiteside smiles sweetly and says, "Now let us tell the Lord about it." Rising from his chair and falling on his knees in the manner of one who habitually spends much time in that attitude, he talks to God as only a very few can.

## The Atmosphere

The visitor senses that God is near. He begins to see his problem from God's perspective. His situation is not as difficult or hopeless as he had thought!

In the hallway of the Home of Peace was a telephone. It rang many times during the day, and often in the middle of the night. Day or night, Mr. Whiteside's patient, courteous "Hello" was ever a comfort to the caller, whether he or she was in another part of the city or possibly in a suburb miles distant.

"Just to hear him say over the phone, 'I will come *at once*,' or, 'We will go to prayer *at once*' gave one such rest and quietness," remembers a woman for whom Whiteside's prayers were God's channel of "power and love and strength."

## The Routine

Each day began early. Quietly the household and guests assembled around the breakfast table—by lamplight in the winter months. Mr. Whiteside's "grace" at meals was usually brief but never perfunctory. It carried those at the table into God's presence, as did all his prayers. Meals were simple but ample and wholesome. Pleasantness and peace sat with those who gathered.

Breakfast over, everyone congregated in the large parlor for morning prayers. These sessions were anything but rote. After a chapter from the Bible, Whiteside would pray or call upon a guest to lead in prayer. Whiteside had many interests on his heart, from sick and distressed people in the city to missionaries abroad who wrote him concerning their work. City, suburbs, state, nation, world—this praying man would carry the minds of all present as he eloquently placed before the Lord this multitude of interests. Then several others would also pray before the group dispersed to their morning tasks.

Nor was this time of household prayer Whiteside's only vigil before the Lord. Only God could have numbered the many, many hours of private intercession. Often Whiteside prayed far into the night; often he rose early and prayed until daybreak. Sometimes he prayed all night. Each day had in it some crisis that called for this man's prayer of faith. Each problem was a call to prayer. Each enterprise, whether his own or someone else's brought to his attention, he spread before the Lord for His blessing and enabling.

## The Clientele

Spiritually and physically broken people visited the home. God accomplished miracles of grace through prayer. Ministers of many communions called on Whiteside for counsel and prayer and went away with renewed vision and stronger faith. Poor human derelicts stopped by the Home. Daddy and Mother Whiteside gave them the loving ministry of the compassionate Christ. One day such a person came to the door. Whiteside answered the bell. After sharing the gospel with the homeless man, he led him to a basement bathroom for a bath. He instructed the man to put his filthy, tattered clothes outside the door, promising him clean apparel in exchange.

When the dirty clothing appeared, Whiteside duly scooped the rags into the furnace and proceeded upstairs to get the substitute clothing he had in mind. Unknown to him, however, while he was out, Annie had given those clothes to another vagrant. Whiteside never owned many suits at a time. Undisturbed, he took his "second best" down to the fortunate tramp waiting in the basement.

The home on Penn Avenue, first at 940, then at 947, had to give way to business interests that built on the sites. Mr. and Mrs. Whiteside moved from Penn Avenue to Stockton Avenue on Pittsburgh's North Side and still later to 320 Cedar Avenue. From this last, Annie went to her eternal home.

Assisted by faithful colleagues, Whiteside carried on for some years longer until his declining strength made such a ministry no longer practical.

## The Praying Man's Praying Wife

Annie Whiteside was E.D. Whiteside's praying partner. They lived in such harmony of ideals and purposes that it is difficult to think of one apart from the other.

"You know," Whiteside remarked one day to a young man still seeking a life partner, "Mrs. Whiteside and I are like two peas in a pod."

Mrs. Whiteside was a gracious woman. And her graciousness was not the kind that some people put on for parlor company, like a new dress, and take off for something different before they enter the kitchen or the laundry. It was the kind that adorns the heart and shines as beautifully among pots and pans as in easy chairs on soft carpeting.

Annie's graciousness stood the tests to which it was often put. It is not possible to do this woman full justice. Annie was a princess, a true daughter of Sarah, a member of heaven's own aristocracy. Perhaps a few word sketches of her sweet, Christlike life will at least suggest the measure of her worth.

## "Full of Grace . . ."

The occasion is special. The Home is expecting an unusually large company of guests for dinner. They have come from a distance for the midweek afternoon meeting held in the Home's chapel.

The meeting is over, and Mrs. Whiteside has been entertaining her guests. She does not resort to small talk. That would muffle the sound of God's voice heard in the meeting. Rather, the sympathetic touches of her words and her personal interest have served to climax what has gone before. Each person senses that the time together has drawn him or her closer to the Lord.

Mrs. Whiteside excuses herself to check on dinner preparations in the kitchen. Several young women are at work, anxious to have the meal ready at the appointed hour. Orderliness and punctuality are the standards in this home where Christ rules. Most of these young women are preparing for the Lord's service in North America or abroad. They love Mrs. Whiteside, and the older woman in turn is like a tender mother to them. If the mealtime guest list is not too long, she presses them to sit at the table with all who are there. She introduces them as lovingly and grandly as if they were guests themselves. Their love for Annie Whiteside and their love for Jesus cause them to be joyful as they work.

But on this occasion something is momentarily wrong. The pudding for dessert has somehow got spoiled—some wrong ingredient has made it inedible.

The young woman responsible for the mistake is full of confusion and remorse. But Mrs. Whiteside's pleasantness is the same as if all were well. And it is not a strained pleasantness. She comforts this child of God who is in one of those little troubles that for the moment can seem so big. Mrs. Whiteside's presence makes the girl forget the worst of it. The meal is served as if all had gone well in its preparation.

## *. . . and Truth"*

Those who knew Annie Whiteside and had the honor of sitting sometimes at that table can see her yet as she smilingly watched for the comfort and enjoyment of all at the table, serving others with no thought of herself, seeing that no one was forgotten if his or her plate seemed to need a second helping. Her motherly attention was ever on the alert.

Once it was too alert for the comfort of one young man in the Home. He was not eating his supper with his usual good appetite. Mother Whiteside asked if he was feeling up to par. His evasive reply caused her to probe more deeply. He finally felt compelled to admit he had that afternoon dulled the edge of his hunger with a piece of watermelon and an ice cream soda!

In those days such indulgences were very rare, and it took all the courage the fellow could muster to tell on himself in the presence of the assembled family! But dear Mrs. Whiteside saw his confusion and suffered with him and did all that Christian courtesy could do to make him forget his embarrassment. In later years he could look back to that episode as worth all it cost him—the price of the soda and the water-melon was but a small part—because of the new understanding it gave him of Mrs. Whiteside's Christlike character.

## Faithful Helpmate

From the time of their marriage on, Annie Whiteside was a willing and faithful partner with her husband in the ministry. It is hard to imagine two workers better matched. Mrs. Whiteside shared with her husband all the trials and tests necessary to make a great prayer warrior and personal evangelist. When the Lord spoke to E.D. Whiteside about opening a mission in the slums of Pittsburgh, obedience did not test his marriage. Annie entered wholeheartedly into the venture. For five years they occupied a single room one floor above the slum mission and one floor below a lodge hall. There was no lack of either noise or smoke. But from Mrs. Whiteside came no complaints.

To all who needed her, Annie Whiteside was a strong tower. On one occasion, during an all-night prayer meeting, Mr. Whiteside fell prostrate on the floor, "to all appearance lifeless." Immediately, Annie was "kneeling at his side, pleading the blood of Jesus, rebuking Satan." The eyewitness adds: "In a few minutes Mr. Whiteside came to, and people helped him to his room. The prayer meeting went on, but it was hard to pray, not knowing if it was Mr. Whiteside's last prayer meeting." Soon, however, he rejoined the group and conducted the meeting through the rest of the night until it ended at 5 in the morning.

Whiteside relied on Annie's counsel. A close acquaintance remarked, "To Mr. Whiteside, her judgment was always right. All she needed to say was, 'Edward, be careful.' That settled the question." Often she accompanied her husband when he went to distant cities to help in Bible conferences and missionary conventions. But whether she was with him or not, their hearts were one in love and devotion to Christ and to each other.

## Final Days

In her last days, Annie was suddenly stricken with paralysis. Annie Frese, a young woman who had lived for a time in the Home with the Whitesides, left a fine prospect and hurried to her side. "I must go to Mother Whiteside," Annie Frese said, "for I owe all I am and have to her." Miss Frese devotedly cared for Mrs. Whiteside until her home going, some two years later.

To lose a lifetime partner under any circumstances is a heavy blow. For Whiteside to lose his loving, sympathetic, always-dependable Annie was particularly devastating. Yet his life was so vitally hidden in Christ and lived so totally in the supernatural that he met this great exigency in triumph. To a missionary friend who had sent him condolences he wrote:

> The home going of my wife was so unexpected and so sudden that I just refused to question the Lord, for I dared not reason. The blow was so great that I dared not trust in my willpower to meet it bravely. Instead, I put my

trust wholly in Jesus. I looked steadfastly past Annie to Jesus Himself. The instant Annie breathed her last breath, Jesus held me as still and calm as though she had only gone to sleep. . . . In place of my wife was Jesus, the gentle Jesus, the sympathetic Jesus. Peace, deep and satisfying, held sway.

On an earlier occasion, Whiteside remarked about his wife to a member of the Home: "I expect to see Mrs. Whiteside very near to the Lord Jesus when we get home to heaven."

It would be five more years before Whiteside would rejoin his beloved wife in the heavenly presence of their Lord and Savior, Jesus Christ.

## Daddy Whiteside's "Boys"

E.D. Whiteside was a trainer of Christian men for Christian service. His method was rare, but it was the method of Elijah, the method of Paul and preeminently the method of Jesus Christ Himself. Elijah trained Elisha by having him with him. Paul trained Timothy and others by having them with him. The Lord Jesus trained His disciples by having them with Him. In the same way Whiteside trained young men for Christian service.

No record has been kept as to how many were thus associated with Whiteside. Certainly it would reach to scores in the course of his lifetime. Commented one person well acquainted with Whiteside's training method:

If it were possible to have before us . . . all those who have been . . . trained for the service of the Lord under the ministry of our dear Brother Whiteside, we should have a very large company.

They later could be found ministering to congregations throughout Pittsburgh and western Pennsylvania as well as on overseas mission fields.

## A One-man School

Whiteside was in himself a whole school of practical Christian work. A number of his students lived for a season in his own home. He observed them. He studied how they spent their time, noted how they prayed, watched their general deportment. At times he had them accompany him to churches where he was ministering. He appointed them to pastorates, and then he telephoned members of the congregation to see how they were doing. At suitable occasions he would get his student workers alone and, on the basis of his findings, advise, counsel and instruct them.

To at least one of these workers he was especially forthright: "The trouble with you is you don't pray enough!" It was a pungent remark, but it proved salutary.

James S. Moore, long associated with Whiteside and his work in Pittsburgh, commented:

He was greatly used of God in preparing young men for the ministry, and many of the

91

Nyack [College] students passed through his hands. He taught them the art of prayer, to wait upon God and to get their messages on their knees. They will rise up in eternity and call him blessed.

Nor was out of sight out of mind. By correspondence, Whiteside continued his contact with those whom he had discipled. One of these was August Helfers, a missionary to India. A letter dated November 7, 1924 reads this way:

Dear Brother Helfers:

Your very kind and comforting letter to hand. Thank you for the information and encouragement your letter contained. Nothing else has such a hopeful aspect as your increasing devotion to the Lord. A love of prayer is the thermometer of spirituality. Cultivate that at any cost. Nothing promotes fruit-bearing like persistent intercession. Nothing provokes Satan so much as faithful united prayer among God's children. Lack of prayer evidences Satan's subtle power, in workers at home or abroad, who substitute other means of fruit-bearing. . . .

Most heartily your brother in Christ,
E.D. Whiteside

## Prayer Was Paramount

Whiteside advised the young men associated with him in the Lord's work to spend hours each day in prayer—"a minimum of three hours." He hardly ever wrote a letter—and he wrote hundreds of letters—without admonishing to prayer and the study of God's Word. They were letters freighted with blessing.

Whiteside never separated prayer from Bible study. To pray without the study of God's Word creates fanatics; to study the Word intellectually and without much prayer creates cold theologians, likely to preach the Word in the killing letter and without the life-giving Spirit. Whiteside was sane and poised; he himself kept these two important matters in proper balance. Thus he had the right to speak to others. He backed every utterance with a consistent and corresponding life. All his words were warm with the love of Christ. Sometimes they cut like a surgeon's scalpel, but always they were loving and tender.

The secret? Christ lived within Whiteside and taught him.

## Carnegie Hall: The Open Reward of Prayer

Carnegie Music Hall on Pittsburgh's North Side has had its full share of important public gatherings. Rapt audiences have filled its tiered seats to marvel as the world's greatest musicians performed. Renowned scientists have lectured prestigious gatherings of scholars. Statesmen speaking there have stirred the fires of patriotism.

At Carnegie Hall, too, the humble, blood-washed children of God, "the aristocracy of heaven," have met in sweetest fellowship. With glowing hearts they have worshiped the consciously present Lord in their midst. In that building the Lord has led them, by means of His Spirit-taught and Spirit-anointed servants, to the fountain of truth. He has given them visions of higher ground in the heavenlies with Christ. From that place He has sent them forth to fight the good fight of faith in an unbelieving world. Panoplied with His armor, they have borne witness to a God who still communes with trusting people. He is a God who lifts their burdens, forgives their sins, heals their sick bodies and resolves the everyday problems of their humdrum lives.

Among the shining names within this category, none in the early years of the twentieth century stood so tall as E.D. Whiteside. To him as God's channel, a multitude of people owe the greatest blessing that has ever come into their lives—blessing which had its origin in the annual Bible and missionary conventions in Carnegie Music Hall.

## A Behind-the-Scenes Presence

Yet a person might have attended those conventions without either seeing or hearing the name Whiteside. He or she might have met God there, receiving His salvation or healing or the anointing of His Spirit without knowing that the human organizer and leader of the great gathering was Whiteside. His humility was such that he shunned publicity. He shunned it because he longed to have people think only of the Lord Jesus and see *Him* and hear *Him* and love *Him*. But let a contrite sinner come forward, or someone sighing for healing, or one seeking God's fullness, and none was as ready as Whiteside to kneel by that person and inspire his or her trembling confidence. Then he would lay gentle hands of love upon the seeker's head and plead in sure and eloquent terms the grace of God for his or her particular need. What power was in those prayers!

As this priest of the sanctuary entered the holiest of all, carrying with him the one for whom he was pleading, the Lord heard and delivered. Then the tears of love and joy would flow as another person found emancipation from bondage and gazed with new wonder on the marvelous provision of God's grace. And Whiteside, glad for one more victory for Jesus our Lord, would utter a quiet, fervent "Hallelujah!"

## A "Sweet and Holy" Atmosphere

The atmosphere of Carnegie Hall on those convention occasions was sweet and holy, like that of a consecrated cathedral. Carnegie Hall was for the moment a real temple of God where the Lord Jesus was preached and honored and worshiped. What made it thus? Whiteside's prayers of faith. Weeks before the convention, Whiteside and his loyal coworkers spent long vigils in prayer. They pleaded God to make Carnegie Music Hall His temple for the convention days. They petitioned Him to drive out all adverse powers that might have found a foothold there.

How shall we tell of the broad influence and the many lives permanently changed through those prayer-wrought conventions? From all over Pittsburgh—North Side, South Side, East End, Wilkinsburg—people came. From the many suburbs and surrounding communities—Homestead, Duquesne, Sewickly, Carnegie, New Castle, Beaver Falls, Butler, Gibsonia, Bakerstown, Valencia, McKees' Rocks, McDonald, Greensburgh, Jeanette, Johnstown, Altoona, Franklin, Oil City—people came. They came from eastern Ohio and from many other places near and far. They came *in answer to prayer* to fill Carnegie Hall during convention days. And God in turn filled their hearts with the good things He had prepared for them at this vestibule of heaven.

Those who spoke during the convention were similarly there because God had brought them there in answer to prayer. Whiteside would pray and the Lord would show him one by one the personnel who were to be convention speakers. It was the Lord's convention, and Whiteside was pleased when those who came to help in the meetings recognized it as such. Some of these speakers were of national fame. Some were missionaries from the ends of the earth. Some were Pittsburgh figures. Some came from other communions than Whiteside's. But all of them were men and women whose hearts the Lord had anointed. And the evangelists bore testimony that they never had spoken where it was "so easy to preach," where they felt that prayer had so thoroughly prepared the way for their messages.

## The Conventions Attracted Sinners

Many were the unsaved who attended, and varying were the motives that brought them. Some came through mere curiosity. Some came because it had been noised abroad that God was in the place. Some were strangely drawn in spite of themselves. But whatever the method or the circumstances, God convinced them as they heard the good news of His love. His Spirit convicted them of sin. Many found their way to the front of the great auditorium to kneel with broken and contrite hearts before the Lord. There God received them into His arms of love. From that moment they began to walk with Him.

God used Whiteside to emphasize the neglected truth of divine healing—Christ's resurrection life for our redeemed bodies, the earnest of our full redemption in the coming age. But always that message was held in perspective. To find Christ in salvation was the greatest discovery a person could make. And God is prepared to fill with His Spirit and give a life of victory and fruitful service the person who surrenders totally to Him and His purposes. That truth also had its due place in the Carnegie conventions. Many thought that they "got it all at conversion" and were prejudiced against the teaching of the Spirit-filled life as an advanced walk of faith. But glowing testimonies in the afternoon "prayer and praise hour" coupled with compelling preaching by men of God disarmed the prejudice. Many surrendered all to Christ and were filled with God's very presence—the only provision He makes for satisfying the human heart that He has created for Himself.

## A Bible and Missionary Convention

The glorious hope of the Lord' return was set forth in song and sermon. It had a direct bearing on the convention's other objective: missions. Those who had been so singularly blessed during the week of conference must have an outlet for the new life now surging within them. There must be a God-given way to express their peace and joy. That, too, Whiteside and his faithful colleagues had prayed over long before the convention days. The closing Sunday was in every sense, the climax of the week.

Often the preceding night, Whiteside and others would spread before the Lord of the harvest the need for consecrated laborers to work in His harvest fields and the need of money to send them out and support them. They would ask God to bless the prayer and praise hour that began the morning, to anoint His messenger in the hour following, to empower and direct the missionary speakers and to move the hearts of His children to give worthily and pledge believingly and sacrificially toward the missionary offering.

Albert B. Simpson, whose missionary passion was already well-known in Christian circles, regularly concluded the conventions. As this mighty man eloquently poured forth the burden of God's missionary heart, people were brought face-to-face with the fact that they were their brothers' keepers. *Not* to sacrifice for world evangelization was a sin.

As Simpson's message concluded, ushers distributed cards on which people could make, over the year that followed, a "faith promise" of money for world evangelization. The form neither carried nor implied any legal obligation. No one would ever ask the donors for the money. These were love promises backed by faith, and over the years very few of them went unfulfilled. In fact, the pledges were regularly oversubscribed.

## Cheerful Givers

In an era when wages were a few dollars a week, the faith offerings at some conventions reached $40,000. Each pledge (but never the name of the donor) was read out amid exclamations of praise and songs of joy. To those who heard the amounts of the pledges without understanding the impelling power behind them, it all seemed improbable. It was sometimes rumored that A.B. Simpson's eloquence had hypnotized his audience! But in the months that followed, the money came in, with hundreds and even thousands of dollars to spare. Paul's words had still the Lord's faithfulness behind them: "God loveth a cheerful giver" (2 Corinthians 9:7).

## The Praying Warrior

Many Christians are not good soldiers. They have never been near enough to the battlefront to hear the enemy's roar of rage. They are so far from the firing line that they hardly recognize the source of a stray, nearly spent bullet when it hits them. But those who follow Christ closely find themselves in the thick of the fight.

During the nearly forty years of his work in Pittsburgh and for years before that, Whiteside was a loyal, valiant soldier of Jesus Christ. He wore the defensive pieces of "the whole armor of God." (See Ephesians 6:11-18.) He was mighty, through God's enabling, in using "the sword of the Spirit, which is the word of God." And he was mighty in prayer.

Whiteside's spiritual faculties were acute and active. He could sense spiritual danger and the need for watchfulness when others were too dull to be apprehensive. Many were the battles he fought and won in the name of the great Commander of the Lord's Army. (See Joshua 5:14.) Often he fought alone, sometimes in company with others. But he was a frontline warrior.

## He Inspired Others

Whiteside's faith and courage inspired the spirits of his comrades and enabled them to win with him. Here is an exhortation he wrote to one fellow soldier:

> Satan cannot accomplish his purposes unless we give in to him. When we yield to doubt, fear, reason or the weakness of indecision, God will not give us victory. He has provided deliverance, and it is always available. I trust that you will not yield to human reason in the present crisis. Human reason is wholly wrong.
>
> You have begun to . . . throw the force of

your willpower on God's side. Keep that up, for it is the secret of ultimate victory and complete healing. Any other course will mean defeat. You and I are on Redemption Highway. This is a supernatural way. The privileges on this road are for "the redeemed of the Lord." That means they are available only to saints. It means they are for those redeemed from the hand of the enemy and the curse of the law. You must avail yourself of your guaranteed rights with a bolder faith—faith in your heavenly Father's Word and in His promises for the body. Reliance upon His faithfulness will honor Him, defeat the already conquered enemy and result in spiritual and physical health (John 16:33; 1 John 5:4; Hebrews 11:11; Galatians 3:13-14; Ephesians 6:13).

The puzzling question is how to make these truths real! Jesus answers briefly, "I am the way" (John 14:6). Put Him before you. Look at Him. Do not take your gaze from Him and put it on anyone else. He is a reality. He will not fail you. Do not try to feel something. Rest on Him. " 'Roll thy' way upon the Lord; trust upon Him; and He worketh" (Psalm 37:5, Young).

God's love for you cannot be measured. The sin of the Israelites was, "They . . . limited the Holy One of Israel" (Psalm 78:41). Your worth to God cannot be estimated, for "As the Father has loved me, so have I loved you," Jesus said of you (John 15:9).

101

## He "Battled on His Knees"

One of Whiteside's good friends recalled the man with these words:

> Mr. Whiteside knew the secret of battling on his knees. He won many glorious conquests at the place of prayer. We all pray, no doubt, but probably few, if any, practice what they preach more than he. On his heart he bore the entire world in intercession.

Ella E. Bird, a Baltimore musician whose consecrated voice, along with that of her sainted sister, brought blessing and victory to hundreds of lives, said this:

> For many years my sister and I were privileged to be associated with the Whitesides in the Lord's work. . . . We fought in many of the same battles against the power of the darkness of this world and rejoiced together in the triumphs of the Lord's glorious cause. . . .
>
> Brother Whiteside possessed a tenacious faith, a faith that took hold with no intention of giving up until his claim was realized. Nothing daunted him in the face of seeming impossibilities. And God honored him. He proved that "with God all things are possible" (Matthew 19:26). I have seen both Brother and Sister Whiteside under the severest of tests, yet always true and triumphant.

The best soldiers are the most likely to draw the enemy's fire. Satan's snipers were on duty constantly to destroy this saintly warrior. Except for God's protection he would long before have been laid low. Let those who would emulate his example study what he once wrote to a woman being assailed by the fiery darts of the wicked one:

> Satan does not have power over us beyond what we through unbelief allow him to have. It is possible to make him run and run very fast. It is possible to cause him suddenly to disappear. "Submit yourselves, therefore to God. Resist the devil, and he will flee from you" (James 4:7).
>
> "Pray without ceasing. In every thing give thanks: for this is the will of God in Christ Jesus concerning you" (1 Thessalonians 5:17-18). "For this purpose the Son of God was manifested, that he might destroy the works of the devil" (1 John 3:8). That applies to the personal experience of every one of God's children.
>
> This salvation is bigger and more wonderful than we have ever realized. The more we trust God and the more fully we yield our wills to His will, the greater and richer are the peace and victory we find in Jesus.

## The Victory Side

Toward the end of his life, Whiteside increasingly emphasized the victory side of life and ignored Satan.

This was so even when he was in the midst of actual spiritual conflict. A few months before he died, a friend called to pray with him.

"You are not feeling very well today, Brother Whiteside," the friend observed.

"No," Whiteside agreed, "I am all knocked out today."

"I'm very sorry," the friend commiserated.

Whiteside sat up quickly, a strange fire in his eyes. "Well, *I* am not sorry," he answered emphatically. "I wouldn't give the devil the pleasure of knowing that I am concerned about my physical condition. Every waking hour I am praising God for my weak condition."

Whiteside believed that praise was a part of the soldier's panoply. Praise, he was convinced, inspires faith in the person who utters it. Annie McFedries, who lived for many years with the Whitesides, said she always knew when Whiteside was in an especially severe spiritual conflict. At those times he was unusually vocal with praise. Praise was an integral part of his battle equipment.

To his last breath, Whiteside was a good soldier. R.F.C. Schwedler was at his side most of the final eight days. He reported:

> Most of that time, except the last three days when he sank into a coma, Mr. Whiteside poured out his soul in intercession. Such travailing in unceasing prayer, such pleading, such intimacy with God I had never before

been privileged to hear. There was no loud crying, no straining, no raising of the voice. But in soft, mellow, modulated tones, he poured out his soul before God. We who were present knew God was harkening and answering. Heaven could not resist those appeals.

The end came quietly for the seventy-eight-year-old veteran. On August 8, 1927, Jesus pronounced His "Well done, good and faithful servant!" and Edward Drury Whiteside took leave of earth to share his heavenly Master's happiness.

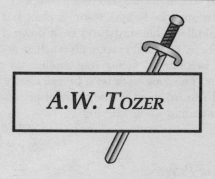

## A.W. TOZER

### A Man of Prayer

*"A twentieth-century prophet" they called him even in his own lifetime. For thirty-one years he was pastor of Southside Alliance Church in Chicago, where his reputation as a man of God was citywide. Concurrently, he became editor of* Alliance Life, *a responsibility he fulfilled until his death in 1963. His greatest legacy to the Christian world has been more than forty books.*

*The following is taken from chapter 12 of* In Pursuit of God, the Life of A.W. Tozer *by James L. Snyder, (Camp Hill, PA: Christian Publications, Inc., 1991.)*

"**P**raying with Tozer was a unique experience. I was delighted the first time he invited me to join him in his study for a time of prayer. After discussing some portion of Scripture over which he recently had been meditating, he suggested we pray. As a much younger man, I waited to see what posture he would take in order that I might comply.

"To my surprise he rose from his chair and stepped to the middle of his study and knelt down. I did the same. There, kneeling erect with no chair or table for support, we prayed facing one another for the next half hour. Thinking back now I recall clearly that the physical feat involved in the spiritual exercise left no room for mental woolgathering."

Robert Walker
*Leaning into the Wind*

## A Man of Prayer

During a business session at a Christian and Missionary Alliance General Council, the delegates were bogged down in motions and amendments and amendments to amendments. Tozer became increasingly impatient with the tedium of it all. Finally, his restless spirit could take no more. He turned to Raymond McAfee sitting beside him.

"Come on, McAfee," he whispered, "let's go up to my room and pray before I lose all my religion."

Whatever acclaim he earned as an eloquent preacher and an outstanding writer can accurately be attributed to his close relationship with God. Tozer preferred God's presence to any other. The foundation of his Christian life was prayer. He not only preached prayer but practiced it. He always carried with him a small notebook in which he jotted requests for himself and others, usually of a spiritual nature.

Tozer's prayers bore the same marks as his preaching: honesty, frankness, humor, intensity. His praying deeply affected his preaching, for his preaching was but a declaration of what he discovered in prayer. His praying also affected his living. He often said, "As a man prays, so is he." Everything he did flowed from his prayer life.

The bulk of his time each day was spent wrestling with God in prayer. Tozer literally practiced the presence of God. Often he would withdraw from family and friends to spend time alone with God. It was not unusual for him to lose all track of time in those meetings with God.

McAfee regularly met in Tozer's study each Tuesday, Thursday and Saturday morning for a half hour of prayer. Often when McAfee would enter, Tozer would read aloud something he recently had been reading—it might be from the Bible, a hymnal, a devotional writer or a book of poetry. Then he would kneel by his chair and begin to pray. At times he prayed with his face lifted upward. Other times he would pray totally prostrated on the floor, a piece of paper under his face to keep him from breathing carpet dust.

## God's Presence

McAfee recalls one especially memorable day.

Tozer knelt by his chair, took off his glasses and laid them on the chair. Resting on his bent ankles, he clasped his hands together, raised his face with his eyes closed and began: "O God, we are before Thee." With that there came a rush of God's presence that filled the room. We both worshiped in silent ecstasy and wonder and adoration. I've never forgotten that moment, and I don't want to forget it.

On occasions while McAfee was praying, he would hear Tozer rustling about. Opening an eye to see what was going on, he would discover Tozer, pencil in hand, writing. While McAfee was praying, Tozer had a thought he wanted to capture.

Tozer met with his church staff regularly for prayer. Once, during a staff prayer meeting, Tozer was prone on the floor in deep conversation with God. The telephone rang. Tozer broke off his prayer to answer the phone. He carried on about a twenty-minute conversation with a pastor giving him all sort of instructions and advice that he himself never followed—taking time off, going on a vacation and so on. The staff just sat there listening and chuckling to themselves because Tozer never took a vacation in his life.

Hanging up the telephone Tozer resumed his position on the floor and picked up where he left off by saying, "Now, God, as I was saying. . . ."

Once Dr. Louis L. King, Tozer and two other preachers were engaged in a half day of prayer. One of the preachers was known for his bombastic, colorful speech both in his preaching and his praying. This man began praying for a certain world leader who at the time was hindering missionary work. "If you can't change him," the preacher prayed, "then kill him and take him to heaven!" Later Tozer took King aside. "Did you hear what he prayed this morning?" he asked, a hurt expression on his face. " 'Take him to heaven'? Why, he doesn't even believe in Jesus Christ. That wasn't prayer. He was saying that for our benefit. You never speak to God in that fashion. When you approach God you should always use reverent language. It's God, not man, we're talking to in prayer!"

## A Sacred Occupation

Prayer, according to Tozer, was the most sacred occupation a person could engage in. Often when Tozer prayed people felt as though God was right at his elbow. Sometimes they were tempted to open their eyes to see.

Tozer's praying embraced the minutiae as well as the transcendental. One time, while King was visiting, Tozer had to go downtown to buy some special lightbulbs for the church. Before the two men left the office Tozer had them both kneel. In the most simple terms, he prayed, "Now, Lord, we don't know anything about lightbulbs." And on he went in a very human way to ask God for wisdom in such a mundane matter as the purchase of lightbulbs.

Summer Bible camps and conferences were a special delight to Tozer. Every year he spent considerable time ministering at these places. To him, the whole atmosphere was conducive to prayer and getting closer to God.

He usually would walk out each morning to the surrounding woods to find a place to pray. Kneeling beside a fallen log he would spend time in worship and prayer. On occasions another person would join him in these rustic prayer meetings. As they began Tozer would have some word to say about coming into the presence of God, which to him was always very real and immediate. Then he would invariably say, "Well, what shall we pray about?" Then followed a brief time of talking about subjects of prayer. Usually Tozer prayed first.

One morning the rain changed his usual plans so he and Robert W. Battles, a close friend, met in Tozer's cabin for prayer at 9 o'clock. Dr. Battles was sharing the conference platform with Tozer. Each knelt on opposite sides of a cot.

"Well, Junior," Tozer asked, "what should we pray for today?"

"I think we should pray for these people who have come to hear the likes of us preach."

The two men talked about prayer and what and who they should be praying for. Then Tozer began to talk about God, the incarnation, the glory and majesty of the Trinity, holiness, heaven, angels, immortality, the church and its mission in the world. No agenda, no sense of time, only the marvelous sense of the presence of God.

Then, before they got around to actually praying, the lunch bell rang.

"Oh, no!" Battles complained. "We didn't even get down to praying and the bell has rung for lunch!"

"Well, Junior. We met to pray. Do you know something? What we have been doing all morning has been perilously close to praying."

There were times as the two men tramped through the nearby woods for a quiet walk together that Tozer would get a far-off look in his eye, his nostrils would flare and he would say in all solemnity, "Junior, I want to love God more than anyone in my generation."

At least once, Tozer lost all track of time as he was in his cabin praying. Time came for him to speak and he was nowhere to be found. Another person had to substitute for him. When Tozer finally did show up, he would only say that he had a more important appointment.

## Focus on God

In prayer Tozer would shut out everything and everyone and focus on God. His mystic mentors taught him that. They showed him how to practice daily the presence of God. He learned the lesson well.

Prayer for Tozer was inextricably tied to worship. "Worship," said Tozer in an uncharacteristically long sentence, "is to feel in your heart and express in some appropriate manner a humbling but delightful sense of admiring awe and astonished wonder and overpowering love in the presence of that most ancient Mystery, that majesty which philosophers call the First Cause but which we call our Father in heaven."

Worship was the impetus behind all he was and did. It controlled every aspect of his life and ministry. "Labor that does not spring out of worship," he would admonish, "is futile and can only be wood, hay and stubble in the day that shall try every man's work."

Rebelling against the hectic schedules that kept his fellow ministers and fellow Christians from true worship, Tozer wrote, "I am convinced that the dearth of great saints in these times, even among those who truly believe in Christ, is due at least in part to our unwillingness to give sufficient time to the cultivation of the knowledge of God. . . . Our religious activities should be ordered in such a way as to leave plenty of time for the cultivation of the fruits of solitude and silence."

Tozer was an ardent lover of hymns and had in his library a collection of old hymnals. Often, on his way to an appointment he would meditate on one of the old hymns.

"Get a hymn book," he frequently advised as he counseled people. "But don't get one that is less than a hundred years old!" His Chicago church did not use the denomination's *Hymns of the Christian Life*. Instead, the congregation sang from a River Brethren Church hymnal. Tozer preferred it because it contained more of the great hymns that he loved, and he enjoyed hearing his people sing them.

"After the Bible," he said in an *Alliance Life* article aimed at new Christians, "the next most valuable book is a good hymnal. Let any new Christian spend a year prayerfully meditating on the hymns of Watts and Wesley alone, and he or she will become a fine theologian." Then he added, "Afterward, let that person read a balanced diet of the Puritans and the Christian mystics. The results will be more wonderful than he could have dreamed." This was his personal pattern, year after year.

## Tozer-gram

If one-tenth of one percent of the prayers made in any American city on any Sabbath day were answered, the world would see its greatest revival come with the speed of light. We seem to have gotten used to prayers that produce nothing. God still hears prayer and all the promises are still good, yet we go on at a pretty dying rate. Can someone tell us the answer?

## Prayer

*O God, I have tasted Thy goodness, and it has both satisfied me and made me thirsty for more. I am painfully conscious of my need of further grace. I am ashamed of my lack of desire. O God, the Triune God, I want to want Thee; I long to be filled with longing; I thirst to be made more thirsty still. Show me Thy glory, I pray Thee, that so I may know Thee indeed. Begin in mercy a new work of love within me. Say to my soul, "Rise up, my love, my fair one, and come away." Then give me grace to rise and follow Thee up from this misty lowland where I have wandered so long. In Jesus' Name, Amen.*

"Following Hard after God"
*The Pursuit of God*